T0191726

CONTINUOUS MEDIA DATABASES

edited by

Aidong Zhang
State University of New York at Buffalo, U.S.A.

Avi Silberschatz
Bell Laboratories, U.S.A.

Sharad Mehrotra
University of California at Irvine, U.S.A.

A Special Issue of
MULTIMEDIA TOOLS AND APPLICATIONS
An International Journal
Volume 11, No. 1 (2000)

SPRINGER SCIENCE+BUSINESS MEDIA, LLC

ISBN 978-1-4613-7034-5   ISBN 978-1-4615-4511-8 (eBook)
DOI 10.1007/978-1-4615-4511-8

Library of Congress Cataloging-in-Publication Data

A C.I.P. Catalogue record for this book is available
from the Library of Congress.

Printed on acid-free paper.

MULTIMEDIA TOOLS AND APPLICATIONS

An International Journal

Volume 11, No. 1, May 2000

Special Issue: Continuous Media Databases
Guest Editors: Aidong Zhang, Avi Silberschatz and Sharad Mehrotra

Distributors for North, Central and South America:
Kluwer Academic Publishers
101 Philip Drive
Assinippi Park
Norwell, Massachusetts 02061 USA
Telephone (781) 871-6600
Fax (781) 681-9045
E-Mail <kluwer@wkap.com>

Distributors for all other countries:
Kluwer Academic Publishers Group
Distribution Centre
Post Office Box 322
3300 AH Dordrecht, THE NETHERLANDS
Telephone 31 78 6392 392
Fax 31 78 6546 474
E-Mail <services@wkap.nl>

 Electronic Services <http://www.wkap.nl>

Library of Congress Cataloging-in-Publication Data

A C.I.P. Catalogue record for this book is available
from the Library of Congress.

Printed on acid-free paper.

Guest Editorial: Continuous Media Databases

This special issue on Continuous-media Databases consists of five selected papers from the Eighth International Workshop on Research Issues in Data Engineering: Continuous-Media Databases and Applications (RIDE98), held at Orlando, Florida, February 23–24, 1998.

The need to handle multimedia data in database systems is growing rapidly in many fields, including video-on-demand servers, education and training, Web browsing, information retrieval, electronic commerce, and distributed publishing. To meet these demands, database systems must have the ability to efficiently store, manage, and retrieve multimedia data. However, conventional database systems were not designed with these applications in mind, and as a result are not suitable to handle these type of new applications. Research on continuous-media database brings about a variety of interesting and challenging issues which are being studied by the multimedia database community.

The aim of RIDE98 workshop was to bring out the issues and methods used in designing continuous-media database systems. Six papers presented at the workshop were invited to submit full length articles for possible publication in this special issue of Multimedia Tools and Applications journal. These papers were subjected to a refereeing process and finally, five papers have been selected for publication in this special issue. These papers address a variety of the relevant issues. The article entitled "Incremental Scheduling of Mixed Workloads in Multimedia Information Servers" by Nerjes, Muth, Paterakis, Romboyannakis, Triantafillou and Weikum offers a comprehensive study of various disk scheduling policies for both continuous and discrete data. A novel disk scheduling algorithm is then identified in such environments. The article entitled "Threshold-Based Dynamic Replication in Large-Scale Video-on-Demand Systems" by Lie, Lui and Golubchik addresses dynamic replication of media objects in parallel video-on-demand systems to improve resource utilization. Several effective storage approaches are investigated and experimented. The article entitled "Query Processing Techniques for Multimedia Presentations" by Lee, Sheng, Balkir, Al-Hamdani, G. Özsoyoğlu and Z.M. Özsoyoğlu presents a graphical query language (GVISUAL) for specification of multimedia presentations and the query processing techniques which translates GVISUAL queries to an operator-based language. The article entitled "Design of Multi-user Editing Servers for Continuous Media" by Ghandeharizadeh and Kim studies data placement, buffering, and scheduling techniques in support of multi-user editing servers for continuous media. The article entitled "Super-Streaming: A New Object Delivery Paradigm for Continuous Media Servers" by Shahabi and Alshayeji proposes a new streaming paradigm that utilizes the client side resources in order to improve the system performance. This paradigm enables the server to deliver media objects at a rate higher than their display requirements.

These papers touch upon some key issues in continuous-media database management and provide an idea of the scope and future directions of the research in this important field.

Many other important issues arise in supporting multimedia data types in databases. These include multimedia analysis, multimedia data model, multimedia data synchronization, and content-based similarity retrieval of multimedia data. The scope and the breadth of topics within multimedia database research cannot be covered in a single special issue. Some of the above mentioned additional topics have been investigated in the past in other special issues elsewhere and will no doubt be covered again in future special issues as the field of multimedia database research and development progresses. We hope that you will enjoy reading this special issue.

Aidong Zhang received her Ph.D. degree in Computer Science from Purdue University, West Lafayette, Indiana, in 1994. She is an associate professor in the Department of Computer Science at State University of New York at Buffalo, Buffalo, New York, 14260. Her current research interests include distributed database systems, multimedia database systems, digital libraries, and content-based image retrieval. She is an author of over 50 research publications in these areas. She is a recipient of the National Science Foundation CAREER award. She serves on the editorial boards of the International Journal of Multimedia Tools and Applications, International Journal of Distributed and Parallel Databases, and ACM SIGMOD DiSC (Digital Symposium Collection). She has also served on various conference program committees.

Avi Silberschatz is the director of the Information Sciences Research Center at Bell Laboratories, Murray Hill, New Jersey. Prior to joining Bell Labs, he held a chaired professorship in the Department of Computer Sciences at the University of Texas at Austin. His research interests include operating systems, database systems, and distributed systems. His most recent research has focused on the areas of multimedia storage servers, high-performance databases, real-time rating and billing systems, real-time operating systems, and electronic commerce. Professor Silberschatz is an ACM Fellow. His writings have appeared in numerous ACM and IEEE publications and other professional conferences and journals. He is a co-author of two well known textbooks—Operating System Concepts and Database System Concepts.

Sharad Mehrotra received his B. Tech. in Computer Science and Engineering at IIT, Kanpur, India in 1988 and an M.S. and Ph.D. in Computer Science at the University of Texas at Austin in 1990 and 1993 respectively. Subsequently he worked at MITL, Princeton as a scientist from 1993–1994. From 1994–1998 he worked as an assistant professor in the Computer Science department and at the Beckman Institute at the University of Illinois at Urbana-Champaign. He specializes in the areas of database management, distributed systems, and information retrieval. His current research projects are on multimedia analysis, content-based retrieval of multimedia objects, multidimensional indexing, uncertainty management in databases, and concurrency and transaction management. Funded by the Army Research Laboratory and the NSF, he is building an integrated information retrieval and database management system entitled MARS. With the help of funding from ARL and NASA, he is developing a specialized spatio-temporal database management technology entitled SATURN. Dr. Mehrotra is an author of over 50 research publications in these areas. He is the recipient of the NSF Career Award and the Bill Gear Outstanding junior faculty research award at the University of Illinois at Urbana-Champaign in 1997.

Incremental Scheduling of Mixed Workloads
in Multimedia Information Servers

G. NERJES   nerjes@inf.ethz.ch
Swiss Federal Institute of Technology, Institute of Information Systems, CH-8092 Zurich, Switzerland

P. MUTH   muth@cs.uni-sb.de
University of the Saarland, Department of Computer Science, D-66041 Saarbrücken, Germany

M. PATERAKIS   pateraki@ced.tuc.gr
Y. ROMBOYANNAKIS   rombo@ced.tuc.gr
P. TRIANTAFILLOU   peter@ced.tuc.gr
Technical University of Crete, Department of Electronics & Computer Engineering, Chania, Greece

G. WEIKUM   weikum@cs.uni-sb.de
University of the Saarland, Department of Computer Science, D-66041 Saarbrücken, Germany

Abstract. In contrast to pure video servers, advanced multimedia applications such as digital libraries or teleteaching exhibit a mixed workload with massive access to conventional, "discrete" data such as text documents, images and indexes as well as requests for "continuous data", like video and audio data. In addition to the service quality guarantees for continuous data requests, quality-conscious applications require that the response time of the discrete data requests stay below some user-tolerance threshold. In this paper, we study the impact of different disk scheduling policies on the service quality for both continuous and discrete data. We provide a framework for describing various policies in terms of few parameters, and we develop a novel policy that is experimentally shown to outperform all other policies.

Keywords: multimedia server, disk scheduling, incremental scheduling, SCAN algorithm, mixed workload, mixed traffic, performance evaluation

1. Introduction

1.1. Service quality and server architecture for continuous data load

Quality of service requirements for "*continuous*" *data* like video and audio pose challenging performance demands on a multimedia information server. In particular, the delivery of such data from the server to its clients dictates disk-service deadlines for real-time playback at the clients. Missing a deadline may result in a temporary, but possibly user-noticeable degradation of the playback that we refer to as a "*glitch*". Guaranteeing a specified quality of service then means to avoid glitches or to bound the glitch rate within a continuous data stream, possibly in a stochastic manner (i.e., with very high probability). In addition, an important objective for the server is to maximize the number of continuous data streams that can be sustained by the system without violating the promised glitch rate bound.

For this setting, a specific data placement and disk scheduling method has evolved in the literature as the method of choice [1, 3, 5–7, 17, 25, 26]. A continuous data object, e.g., a video, is partitioned into *fragments* of constant time length, say 1 second of display. These fragments are then spread across a number of disks in a round-robin manner such that each fragment resides on a single disk. Such a coarse-grained striping scheme allows a maximum number of concurrent streams for a single object (i.e., regardless of skew in the popularity of objects), while also maximizing the effective exploitation of a single disk's bandwidth (i.e., minimizing seek and rotational overhead). Furthermore, the fact that all fragments have the same time length makes it easy to support data with variable-bit-rate encoding (e.g., MPEG-2) and simplifies the disk scheduling as follows. The periodic delivery of the fragments of the ongoing data streams is organized in *rounds* whose length corresponds to the time length of the fragments. During each round, each disk must retrieve those of its fragments that are needed for a client's playback in the subsequent round. Not being able to fetch all the necessary fragments by the end of a round is what causes a glitch. On the other hand, since the ordering of the fragment requests within a round can be freely chosen, the disk scheduling can and should employ a SCAN policy [22] (also known as "elevator" or "sweep" policy) that minimizes seek times.

Various analytic models have been developed in the literature for the above scheduling method. Their role is to derive, from the data and disk parameters, the maximum number of concurrent data streams that a single disk can sustain without risking glitches or exceeding a certain probability that glitches become non-negligible. These predictions are based on either worst-case assumptions on the various parameters (e.g., data fragment size, rotational latency of the disk, etc.) [17], or different forms of stochastic modeling (e.g., assuming a probability distribution for the data fragment size) [2, 14, 27]. In the latter case, which is similar to "statistical multiplexing" in ATM switches, a service quality guarantee could take the following form: *the probability that a continuous data stream with r rounds exhibits more than 0.01 * r glitches is less than 0.001.*

For given requirements of this form, the analytic performance model then serves to configure the server (i.e., compute the required number of disks for a given load) and to drive the server's run-time admission control.

1.2. Support for discrete data load and mixed workload service quality

In contrast to pure video servers, advanced applications such as digital libraries or teleteaching exhibit a mixed workload with massive access to conventional, *"discrete" data* such as text documents and images as well as index-supported searching in addition to the requests for continuous data. Furthermore, with unrestricted 24-hour world-wide access over the Web, such multimedia servers have to cope with a dynamically evolving workload where the fractions of continuous-data versus discrete-data requests vary over time and cannot be completely predicted in advance. Thus, for a good cost/performance ratio it is mandatory that a server operates with a shared resource pool rather than statically partitioning the available disks and memory into two pools for continuous and discrete data, respectively.

In addition to the service quality guarantees for continuous data requests, quality-conscious applications require that the response time of the discrete data requests stay below some user-tolerance threshold, say one or two seconds. This requirement has been largely ignored in prior work on multimedia information servers where the performance of discrete-data requests often appears to be an afterthought at best. Among the few exceptions are the Fellini project [10, 17] which allows reserving a certain fraction of a disk service round for discrete data requests, the Cello framework [23] which considers different classes of applications including applications accessing discrete-data, and the Hermes project [15, 16] which has aimed to derive stochastic models to support the configuration of a mixed workload server (i.e., the number of required disks). In the latter approach, a stochastic bound for the continuous-data glitch rate (see above) is combined with a discrete-data performance goal of the following form: *the probability that the response time of a discrete data request exceeds 2 seconds is less than 0.001.*

1.3. Contribution and outline of the paper

While the above mentioned prior work has shown increasing awareness of mixed workloads and a comprehensive notion of service quality, the actual disk scheduling for the two classes of requests has been disregarded or "abstracted away" because of its analytical intractability. In this paper, we study the impact of different disk scheduling policies on the service quality for both continuous and discrete data. In doing so, we use a round-based scheduling paradigm as our starting point, as this is the best approach to deal with discretized continuous data streams. Also, this approach allows us to concentrate on a single disk, for our framework ensures independence among disks and linear scalability in the number of disks. Our focus here is on the details of how continuous and discrete data requests are scheduled within a round. The paper makes the following contributions:

- We identify a number of critical issues in the disk scheduling policy, and present a framework for describing the various policies in terms of few parameters.
- We develop a novel policy, coined *incremental scheduling*, that outperforms all other policies in detailed simulation experiments, and is thus advocated as the method of choice for mixed workload scheduling.
- We describe, in detail, implementation techniques for the incremental scheduling policy, and present a prototype system into which this policy is integrated.

This paper is an extended version of [13]. In [13] we introduced the framework of scheduling policies for mixed workloads, and presented preliminary simulation results. The current paper extends that work by including systematic and comprehensive experimental results, by identifying the incremental policy as the method of choice, and by developing detailed algorithms and implementation techniques for this policy including its integration into a prototype system.

The rest of the paper is organized as follows. Section 2 introduces different issues in the scheduling of mixed workloads, and organizes them into a framework. Section 3 provides a qualitative discussion of the benefits and drawbacks of the various scheduling policies, aiming to prune the space of worthwhile policies. Section 4 presents algorithms and implementation techniques for the most promising scheduling policies. Section 5 contains performance results from a detailed simulation study. Section 6 describes the prototype system into which the incremental scheduling policy is integrated.

2. Scheduling strategies

We consider a single disk which has to serve N concurrent continuous-data streams per scheduling round, and also has to sustain discrete-data requests that arrive according to a Poisson process with rate λ (i.e., exponentially distributed time between successive arrivals, with a mean interarrival time $1/\lambda$). In the following, we refer to fetching a continuous-data fragment as a *C-request* and to a discrete-data request as a *D-request*. The scheduling has several degrees of freedom along the following dimensions:

(1) *Service period policy*: We can either serve C-requests and D-requests together in an arbitrarily interleaved manner (*mixed policy*), or separate the service of C-requests and D-requests into two disjoint periods (*disjoint policy*) within each round. In the latter case, a prioritization of a request class, i.e., C-requests vs. D-requests, is possible by ordering the C-period before the D-period or vice versa. In addition, we can break a round down into a specified number of *subrounds*. Subrounds can again use a mixed policy or can be partitioned into disjoint C- and D-periods.

(2) *Limitation policy*: Only a limited number of C-requests and D-requests can be served in each round. We can either specify a limit on the number of requests of a given class served in a (sub)round (*number limit*), or on the length of the period assigned to each class of requests (*time limit*). The last period in each round is always time-limited by the beginning of the next round.

(3) *Request selection and queue ordering policy*: Within each (sub)round or period, we can select a set of requests to be included into the disk queue (up to a limit as defined in (2)), and arrange them in a specific execution order. Among the many possible ordering criteria discussed in the literature (see, e.g. [4, 22, 28]), a first-come-first-served (*FCFS*) order is reasonable whenever fairness is an issue and the variance of the response time (for D-requests) is critical. On the other hand, a *SCAN* policy minimizes seek overhead and thus achieves better throughput results.

The following Subsections 2.1 through 2.3 discuss these scheduling dimensions in more detail. Subsection 2.4 then puts everything together in organizing the various options into a common framework.

2.1. Service period policy

Given the real-time nature of the C-requests, the most obvious approach is to break down the entire service round into a C-period during which all N C-requests are served, and a D-period for the D-requests. We refer to this policy, which has been assumed (but not further analyzed) in our earlier work [15], as a *disjoint policy*.

Since C- and D-periods always alternate over an extended time period, it may seem that the order of these two periods within a round is not an issue. However, this order has a certain impact on the service quality of the two classes. Namely, picking the C-period as the first part of a service round, the probability of glitches can be minimized or even eliminated by dynamically extending the C-period if necessary and shortening the D-period

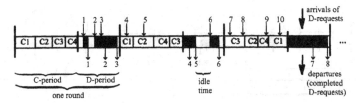

Figure 1. Execution scenario with disjoint C- and D-periods.

accordingly. If, on the other hand, the D-period is placed first, the risk is higher that the C-period needs to be truncated by the end of the round.

Figure 1 illustrates the disjoint policy with the C-period preceding the D-period. Time progresses from left to right. The end of each round is marked by a long vertical line, short vertical lines separate C-periods and D-periods. C-requests are represented as lightly shaded boxes, D-requests as dark shaded boxes. White boxes indicate idle periods with no request served. Each C-period serves $N = 4$ C-requests (in variable order depending, e.g., on seek positions). We show the timepoints when D-requests arrive and when they depart after their execution is completed by means of arcs. D-requests are identified by numbers. The timespan between the arrival and the departure of a D-request is the response time of that request. The figure contains cases where a D-request that arrives during the C-period is delayed until the subsequent D-period, e.g., requests 4 and 5, and also cases where this delay spans more than one round because of a temporary load peak for D-requests (many arrivals and/or large requests and thus long service times), e.g., requests 9 and 10.

The biggest drawback of the 2-period scheme is that it may delay D-requests for a long time. Even if the D-request arrival rate is low (so that there is no real contention among the D-requests), a D-request that has the bad luck to arrive early in the C-period needs to wait for almost the entire C-period. Depending on the total round length and its C-period fraction, such a delay may be user-noticeable. An idea to alleviate this situation is to break down the entire C-period into a fixed number of C-periods and interleave these C-periods with shorter D-periods. We refer to a successive pair of C- and D-period as a *subround*. The difference between a subround and the entire round is that all C-requests need to be served within the round, but only a fraction of them is relevant for a subround. The number of subrounds per round should be a tuning parameter, where the value 1 corresponds to the initial 2-period scheme.

Figure 2 illustrates the disjoint policy with 2 subrounds per round. Note that the more fine-grained interleaving of C- and D-periods on a per subround basis improves the response time of some D-requests, e.g., requests 4 and 5, which now have to wait only for the end of one C-subround-period rather than the C-period of an entire round.

The major alternative to this separation of C- and D-periods is to combine both request classes into a common disk queue, using a *mixed policy*. This approach is beneficial for the D-requests as they have a chance to be served earlier. D-requests that arrive during what used to be the C-period do not necessarily have to wait until the end of the C-period. Whether this is actually the case for a given D-request arrival depends on the details of how requests are ordered in the common disk queue, as discussed in Subsection 2.3.

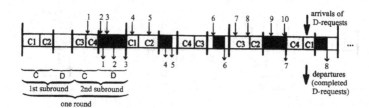

Figure 2. Execution scenario with disjoint C- and D-periods and 2 subrounds per round.

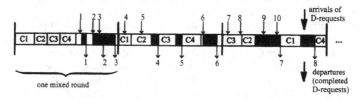

Figure 3. Execution scenario with mixed service periods.

A possible execution schedule for the scenario of figure 1 with a mixed policy is illustrated in figure 3. Note that some of the D-requests, e.g., requests 4 and 5, now have a shorter response time, compared to the execution scenario in figure 1.

2.2. Limitation policy

Only a limited number of C-requests and D-requests can be served in each round. Assigning different limits to each class of requests allows us to tune the system between the two classes. We consider two kinds of limits:

- a *number limit*, i.e., an upper bound for the number of requests of a given class served during a (sub)round
- a *time limit*, i.e., an upper bound for the time available to serve the requests of a given class within a (sub)round.

Number limit. In general, the number of C-requests to be served in a round is number-limited by N. When using subrounds, we distribute the C-requests uniformly over the subrounds. The number N of C-requests should be determined by the admission control so that the total service time for the N C-requests is smaller than the entire round length (or period length if the C-period is time-limited). If the admission control is based on a stochastic model, then this inequality holds with very high probability. In the unlikely event that glitches are inevitable, smoothful degradation policies can be devised along the lines of [9, 24].

Obviously, the resource consumption by D-requests can adversely affect the glitch rate of C-requests as well, down to the point where no guarantees about glitch rates can be given anymore. Therefore, it is advisable that the number of D-requests that are considered for execution within a (sub)round be also limited. Limiting the number of D-requests can be done

- *statically* based on a stochastic model for their disk service time, similar to the admission control of C-requests, or
- *dynamically* by computing the total disk service time for the D-requests at the beginning of each (sub)round.

In the first case, we obtain a static limit which is constant for all rounds until the global load parameters change and the stochastic model is re-evaluated. In the second case, the number limit for D-requests can vary from round to round, depending on the actual request sizes, etc.

Time limit. Instead of imposing a limit on the number of requests served for a given class, we can limit the time spent for serving requests of this class in a round. For example, assuming a round length of 1 second, we could dedicate 0.6 seconds to the C-period and 0.4 seconds to the D-period. Obviously, this only makes sense for the disjoint policy with separate periods assigned to each class. A time limit can be specified based on the desired disk load ratio between C-request and D-requests. Ideally, this ratio would be derived from the specified performance and service quality goals of the application, under the assumption that the disk system configuration is indeed able to satisfy these goals. Configuration methods along these lines have been studied in [15, 16]. In the current paper, we assume the length of the periods to be given.

Analogously to a number-limit specification, the time limit for a service period can be chosen *statically*, i.e., with a fixed upper bound such as 0.6 seconds, or *dynamically* on a per (sub)round basis. In the latter case, for example, the time limit for the D-request service period could be chosen depending on the D-request sizes, the time already consumed by the C-period, etc. Thus, a dynamic time limit essentially has the same flexibility and achieves the same net effect as a dynamic number limit. We therefore unify the two dynamic cases into a *dynamic limitation policy*, where the resulting number and time limits for a round are merely dual views of the same load limitation.

2.3. Request selection and queue ordering policy

At the beginning of each (sub)round, the disk scheduler considers the entire set of requests that are known at this point. According to the limitation policy of Section 2.2, the scheduler first determines a subset of requests to be included into the disk queue for the next (sub)round. We refer to this decision as the *request selection policy*. As for the C-requests, the choice is uncritical as long as all N requests are guaranteed to be scheduled within one of the subrounds of the entire round. For D-requests, we advocate a selection policy based on the arrival time of the requests for fairness reasons. So the subset of "lucky" D-requests should always be chosen in FCFS order. Otherwise, it would be hard if not infeasible to prevent the potential starvation of D-requests.

When the set of requests is selected, the disk scheduler needs to arrange them in a certain service order. In our specific setting, there are two attractive options for this *queue ordering policy*:

- In a SCAN ordering, the requests in the queue are ordered with regard to their disk seek positions, relative to the innermost or outermost cylinder or the current disk arm position. This policy aims to maximize the effectively exploited disk bandwidth by minimizing seek times.
- In a FCFS ordering, requests are ordered based on their arrival time. All C-requests have the same arrival time, namely, the startpoint of the round. The main incentive for a FCFS scheme would be that it provides a certain fairness among requests, often resulting in a smaller variance of the response time compared to other, "unfair" ordering policies.

D-requests may arrive during a (sub)round, and if the given limit on D-requests is not exceeded, it may be beneficial to include them incrementally into the ordering of requests in the (sub)round. We call this an *incremental* queue ordering policy opposed to *non-incremental* queue ordering policies which determine all requests to be served in a (sub)round at the beginning of the (sub)round and postpone the service of request arriving during the (sub)round to the next (sub)round. For incremental queue ordering policies with SCAN ordering, a newly arriving D-request can be merged into the SCAN ordering if its seek position is still ahead of the current disk arm position. Otherwise, the request is either placed at the end of the list of D-requests to be served in the current (sub)round, i.e., after the disk sweep, or it is considered only at the beginning of the next (sub)round. When more than one request is postponed in this manner, one actually needs a subsidiary policy for ordering the postponed requests, provided that they can still be served within the same service period. For simplicity, we assume that this subsidiary policy is the same as the primary queue ordering criterion. So, for SCAN ordering, postponed requests would be combined into a second disk sweep.

A possible caveat that could be brought up with regard to the incremental queue ordering policy is the overhead of the necessary run-time bookkeeping. In particular to reduce the overhead, with a SCAN policy for request ordering, it could make sense to allow dynamically arriving requests to be included for service in the current round only after the current disk sweep is completed. So all requests that arrive during a sweep constitute the set of requests for the next sweep, provided that there is sufficient time left within the round. We refer to this kind of request selection policy as *gated incremental*, as opposed to the fully *incremental* policy outlined above where new requests may be included even in an ongoing disk sweep.

2.4. *Putting everything together*

The various scheduling dimensions that we discussed in the previous subsections can be combined into a common framework where scheduling policies can be described in terms of only few parameters. These parameters and their possible settings are as follows:

(1) A specification for the service period policy. Possible choices are

   (a) disjoint periods with the C-period preceding the D-period,
   (b) disjoint periods with the D-period preceding the C-period,
   (c) mixed periods.

(2) The number of subrounds per round, where 0 denotes a mixed round without separate periods, and 1 corresponds to the standard 2-period case without subrounds.
(3) A specification of the limitation policy. Possible choices are

   (a) a static number limit,
   (b) a static time limit,
   (c) a dynamic limitation for each (sub)round.

(4) A specification of the request selection and queue ordering policy. For the selection of D-requests, we consider only FCFS. For the queue ordering, possible settings are

   (a) SCAN for the C-requests combined with FCFS for D-requests,
   (b) SCAN for the C-requests combined with incremental FCFS for D-requests,
   (c) SCAN for the C-requests combined with SCAN for the D-requests,
   (d) SCAN for the C-requests combined with incremental SCAN for the D-requests,
   (e) SCAN for the C-requests combined with gated incremental SCAN for the D-requests.

3. Qualitative assessment

In this section we briefly discuss the pros and cons of the various scheduling policies that one may construct from the framework of Section 2. Our goal is to restrict the space of "promising" policies to a small set for further experimental study.

First of all, we observe that the dynamic limitation policy, where either the number of requests or the total service time of a service period is chosen dynamically based on request parameters, is strictly superior to a static number or time limit. A possible advantage of the static limitation policies would be that they need no on-line information about current load parameters and can therefore be implemented with virtually no bookkeeping overhead. However, the results of Section 5.6 show that this overhead is negligible. Hence we consider the dynamic limitation as the method of choice.

Second, among the two disjoint service period policies, we favor the one with C-periods preceding D-periods for the following reason. As we do not have a static time limit for the C-period, we can always allow all C-requests of a (sub)round to complete and adjust the remaining D-period dynamically. In other words, the risk of having glitches in continuous-data streams is minimized. So the design decision expresses a prioritization of C-requests over D-requests, and this seems to be in line with the design rationale of most multimedia applications that include video/audio clips.

Finally, we strongly advocate the choice of FCFS for the request selection policy to prevent starvation (as already mentioned in Section 2.3). Furthermore, we can narrow down the space of interesting queue ordering policies by observing that the incremental policies are strictly superior to non-incremental policies, and that the incremental SCAN policy is strictly superior to the gated incremental SCAN policy where the disk-arm sweep consists only of requests that have arrived before the sweep begins.

So altogether, this qualitative discussion leaves us with the following scheduling policies that we consider worthwhile to be studied experimentally:

(a) *Disjoint with dynamically incremental FCFS*: disjoint service periods with the C-period with SCAN service preceding the D-period, a dynamic limitation of D-requests, and incremental FCFS queue ordering for the D-requests,

(b) *Disjoint with dynamically incremental SCAN*: the same policy except that the D-request queue is ordered (and dynamically re-ordered) by the incremental SCAN policy,

(c) *Mixed with dynamically incremental SCAN*: a mixed service period with a dynamic limitation of D-requests and a dynamically incremental SCAN policy for both C- and D-requests,

(d) *Mixed with dynamically gated incremental SCAN*: a mixed service period with a dynamic limitation of D-requests and a gated incremental SCAN policy for both C- and D-requests.

Policy d) is potentially interesting insofar as its overhead for run-time bookkeeping is lower than that of policy c) while one could hope that the performance of the two policies is comparable. Note that for all four policies, the number of subrounds is still a degree of freedom. In this paper, however, we restrict ourselves to setting this parameter to one; so we do not further consider non-trivial subrounds here.

4. Algorithms and implementation techniques

In this section the algorithms for the scheduling policies selected in the previous section are described in more detail. All algorithms make use of two data structures:

(1) a *fifo queue* that contains all D-requests and
(2) a *scan list* in which requests are ordered by increasing cylinder number.

In terms of these data structures, the algorithms can be described as follows:

(a) *Disjoint with incremental FCFS*: At the beginning of a new round the scan list is filled with C-requests that must be processed in this round. The algorithm first determines the scan direction, by choosing among the innermost and the outermost request in the scan list the one that is closer to the current disk arm position. Starting with this request, the algorithm iterates over the scan list. When the service of a request exceeds the end of the current round, remaining C-requests in the list are no longer served in the current round and discarded. When the scan list has been processed completely and there is time left until the end of the round, the processing of D-requests starts. They are processed from the fifo queue until the round expires.

(b) *Disjoint with dynamically incremental SCAN*: The first part of this algorithm is identical to that of the previous algorithm (described in (a)). When there is time left after the service of the C-requests, the scan list is filled with as many D-requests as possible. These D-requests are selected from the fifo queue and inserted into the scan list until the estimated total service time exceeds the remaining time in the current round or the fifo queue has been emptied. Idle time at the end of the current round is avoided by allowing a D-request at the tail of the scan list to possibly spill over into the next round. This is feasible as we still guarantee the service of all C-requests within the current round. After this initial filling, the scan direction is determined as described in (a) and the D-requests are processed. After each service the scan algorithm considers updating the scan list. D-requests are selected from the fifo queue and inserted into the scan list provided that their cylinder position is ahead of the current position of the disk arm in scan direction. This is repeated until the estimated total service time for all requests in the scan list exceeds the remaining time in the current round. When the scan list becomes empty, e.g., when the arrival rate of D-requests is low, the algorithm waits until the arrival of a new D-request and then reinitiates the filling of the scan list with D-requests. Alternatively, if the beginning of a new round occurs first, the algorithm restarts with the handling of C-request as described in (a).

(c) *Mixed with dynamically incremental SCAN*: At the beginning of a new round, all C-requests are inserted into the scan list. Then D-requests from the fifo queue are inserted into the scan list until the estimated total service time for all requests in the scan list exceeds the remaining time in the current round or the fifo queue becomes empty. Like in (b), we allow a D-request at the tail of the scan list to possibly spill over into the next round. Unlike (b), however, it is now possible to have a C-request at the tail of the scan list. In order to avoid glitches, the estimated total service time of the scan must not exceed the round length in this case.

After the initial filling of the scan list, the scan direction is determined as described in (a). Analogously to (b), after each request service, the scan algorithm considers newly arrived D-requests if there is idle time at the end of the round. D-requests are selected from the fifo queue and inserted into the scan list, provided that their cylinder positions are ahead of the current disk arm position in scan direction. This is repeated until the estimated service for all requests in the scan list exceeds the remaining time in the current round. Again a D-request at the tail of the scan list can remain in the list even if it is estimated that the disk sweep exceeds the round length a little bit (i.e., by at most one D-request service). When the scan list becomes empty, the algorithm waits for the arrival of new D-requests and then restarts filling the scan list (but then without any C-requests) or waits for the beginning of the next round.

(d) *Mixed with dynamically gated incremental SCAN*: This algorithm proceeds identically to the previous one described in (c), except that it considers newly arrived D-requests only when a disk sweep completes. Thus, the filling procedure is not invoked after each request service, but only at the beginning of the round and whenever a disk sweep completes and there is still time left in the current round.

All four algorithms can be combined into a single scheduling procedure (*scheduleMixed-Workload*) whose pseudocode is given in figure 4. The fill procedure (*fillScanList*) is outlined in figure 5. It aims to place as many D-requests as possible into the scan list, while still

```
procedure scheduleMixedWorkload() {
  forever {

    fill scan list with C-requests.

    if disjoint policy {
      // service C-requests in the first period of the round
      while (current round not expired
             and ScanList is not empty) {
        process requests of ScanList in direction ScanDirection;
      }
    }

    // loop until round has expired
    while ( current round not expired ) {
      // select queue ordering policy
      switch (queue ordering policy) {

        case dynamically incremental scan policy:
          fillScanList();
          if ( ScanList is not empty)
            process requests of ScanList
              in direction ScanDirection;
          else {
            ScanDirection := undefined.
            wait until current round expires or D-request arrives;
          }
          break;

        case gated incremental scan ordering:
          if ( ScanList is empty )
            fillScanList();
          if ( ScanList is not empty)
            process requests of ScanList
              in direction ScanDirection;
          else {
            ScanDirection := undefined,
            wait until current round expires or D-request arrives;
          }
          break;

        case dynamically incremental fcfs ordering
          if ( FifoQueue is not empty)
            get and process request from FifoQueue;
          else
            wait until current round expires or D-request arrives;
          break,
      }
    }
  }
}
```

Figure 4. Scheduling algorithm.

```
procedure fillScanList() {
  while ( FifoQueue is not empty and
          estimateSvcTime() < time left in current round) {

    req := next request from FifoQueue,

    // ScanDirection is only defined in case of "refill"
    if ( (ScanDirection is not undefined and
          req is ahead of current position) or
          ScanDirection is undefined ) {
      insert req into ScanList;

      // if request causes a glitch, it should not have been inserted
      if ( (estimateSvcTime() > time left in current round)
           and a C-request is at the head or tail of ScanList)
        delete req from ScanList;
      else
        delete req from FifoQueue.
    }
  }
  if ( ScanDirection is undefined )
    determineScanDirection();
}
```

Figure 5. Fill scan list.

16

```
procedure double estimateSvcTime() {
    totalSvcTime := 0;
    tempcyl := current head position;
    if (ScanDirection is undefined)
        determineScanDirection();
    foreach request in ScanList {
        totalSvcTime += seektime between tempcyl
                        and cylinder of request

        if (rotational delay is known)
            totalSvcTime += rotational delay of request;
        else
            totalSvcTime += worst case rotational delay;

        totalSvcTime += size of request / transfer rate of disk;
        tempcyl := cylinder of request;
    }
    return totalSvcTime;
}
```

Figure 6.   Estimate service time.

```
procedure determineScanDirection() {
    frontcyl := cylinder of request from head of ScanList;
    backcyl := cylinder of request from tail of ScanList;
    currentcyl:= current head position;

    // take shortest way to either head or tail of ScanList
    if ( |frontcyl – currentcyl| < |backcyl – currentcyl| ) or
    ( only one request in ScanList and frontcyl > currentcyl)
        ScanDirection := forward;
    else
        ScanDirection := backward;
    }
}
```

Figure 7.   Determine scan direction.

guaranteeing that all C-requests can be served within the current round. To this end, it needs to estimate the total service time required for all request in the scan list. This estimation procedure (*estimateSvcTime*) is given in figure 6. It is based on the perfect knowledge of all seek distances when the scan list has been filled, a sufficiently accurate model of seek times [20], the request sizes, and the transfer rate of the disk (or the disk's various zones in case of a multi-zone disk). The only parameter that is unknown and cannot be accurately estimated at the beginning of a disk sweep is the rotational latency of the requests in the scan list. Thus, this parameter is conservatively estimated by assuming that each request is delayed by a full disk revolution between the completion of the seek and the beginning of the data transfer. We will discuss in Section 5.5 to what extent this conservative bound leads to unutilized disk resources. The final procedural building block to be mentioned here is the procedure for determining the scan direction (*determineScanDirection*) whose pseudocode is given in figure 7.

5. Simulation experiments

5.1.   Testbed

Our testbed uses the process-oriented discrete-event simulation package CSIM+ [11]. This package maintains simulated time and provides support for collecting data during the execution of the model. Furthermore it allows to create processes that are able to run concurrently within the simulated time.

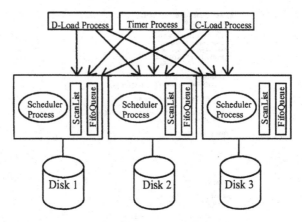

Figure 8. Architecture of the simulation testbed.

Figure 8 shows the setup of the simulation. Each disk has its own *Scheduler Process* that runs the scheduling algorithms described in Section 4 and simulates the specified disk behavior (realistic seek times etc.). Each scheduler has its own set of data structures (*ScanList, FifoQueue*). The *D-Load Process* is responsible for the generation of a Poisson arrival stream of D-requests according to the specified arrival rate. It inserts a randomly generated D-request into the appropriate FifoQueue. The *C-Load Process* assigns a fixed number of C-requests to each scheduler. The *Timer Process* keeps track of the current time and informs all schedulers when a new round begins.

5.2. Parameter values

Our testbed simulates a storage system with five disks. Relevant disk parameters are given in Table 1. These values reflect the characteristics of modern disk drives.

It is assumed that for each disk there is a constant number N of C-requests that must be served in each round. The round length is set to one second, and subrounds are disregarded (i.e., the subround parameter is set to 1). The data characteristics for C- and D-requests are

Table 1. Disk characteristics.

Transfer rate	8.79 MBytes/s
Revolution time	8.34 ms
Seek-time function	
$seek(d) = \begin{cases} 1.867 * 10^{-3} + 1.315 * 10^{-4} \sqrt{d}; d < 1344 \\ 3.8635 * 10^{-3} + 2.1 * 10^{-6} d; d \geq 1344 \end{cases}$	
Number of cylinders	6720

Table 2. Data characteristics for D-requests.

C-request size	Mean $E[S_C]$	800000 Bytes
(Gamma distributed)	Variance $Var[S_C]$	$(200000)^2$
D-request size	Mean $E[S_D]$	50000 Bytes
(Normal distributed)	Variance $Var[S_D]$	$(25000)^2$

given in Table 2. The values for C-requests reflect typical data characteristics of MPEG-2 data with a mean bandwidth of 6.1Mbit/s. The sizes of D-requests are typically smaller and obey a Normal distribution. The arrival of D-requests is driven by a Poisson process with arrival rate λ, and it is assumed that the arriving D-requests are distributed uniformly over the disks.

5.3. Performance comparison of algorithms

We compared the four scheduling policies that we identified as the most promising ones in Section 3:

(a) Disjoint with dynamically incremental FCFS
(b) Disjoint with dynamically incremental SCAN
(c) Mixed with dynamically incremental SCAN
(d) Mixed with dynamically gated incremental SCAN

The performance metrics of interest are the maximum sustainable throughput of D-requests (for a given C-load) and the mean response time of D-requests. All four scheduling policies prevent glitches in C-data streams (unless the C-requests alone exceed the entire round length, which is extremely unlikely for our workload parameter settings and did never occur in the experiments).

Figure 9 shows the mean response times of D-requests for different arrival rates of D-requests and different numbers N of C-requests (3 or 7) to be served in a round. Serving 3 C-requests per round results in about 30% of the total round time occupied by C-requests on average, serving 7 C-requests per round results in about 70%.

Figure 9 shows that the mixed dynamically incremental SCAN policy is superior under all settings. In fact, this clear result is not that unexpected, because this policy does not force D-requests that arrive during the C-period to wait until the end of the C-period. The mixed dynamically gated incremental SCAN policy, however, performs similarly to the disjoint policy with dynamically incremental SCAN. The reason is that in both policies D-requests have to wait for a significant time until a new D-period or a new disk sweep is started.

The maximum sustainable throughput is almost independent of choosing a disjoint or mixed policy. The important parameter here is the queue ordering policy. Using a SCAN policy is superior to FCFS. The reason is that the SCAN policy saves seek time compared to the FCFS policy, which allows more D-requests to be served in a round.

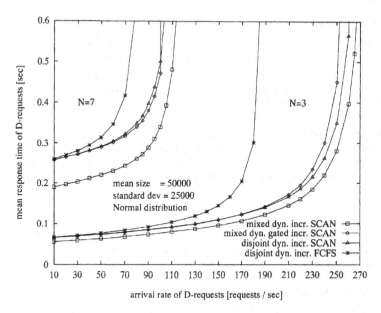

Figure 9.   Mean response time of D-requests.

For low arrival rates of D-requests, the response times of the two policies with disjoint service periods are similar. The reason is that under light D-load, the number of requests in a disk sweep is small. Due to the dynamic and incremental inclusion of newly arriving D-requests into the set of D-requests to be served in a round, a light D-load results in multiple disk sweeps during the round. In the extreme case, the SCAN policy with incremental queue ordering degenerates towards a FCFS policy.

Between the two disjoint-period policies, FCFS did not offer any real benefits in terms of response time variance either. This was not in line with our expectations, but the explanation is that for our workload characteristics seek times were a significant factor of the disk service time per request, and the minor "unfairness" of the SCAN policy was more than made up by the reduction of the disk service time. For much larger requests, where seek times become an insignificant factor, FCFS may outperform SCAN in terms of response time variance, but this would require request sizes in the order of Megabytes.

5.4. Sensitivity studies

To show the robustness of the algorithms with regard to various workload parameters, we investigated the impact of smaller D-request sizes or higher variances. Furthermore we generated also Gamma distributed D-request sizes to study the impact of other distribution functions.

20

Table 3.   Data characteristics for small D-requests.

C-request size	Mean $E[S_C]$	800000 Bytes
(Gamma distributed)	Variance $Var[S_C]$	$(200000)^2$
D-request size	Mean $E[S_D]$	10000 Bytes
(Normal distributed)	Variance $Var[S_D]$	$(5000)^2$

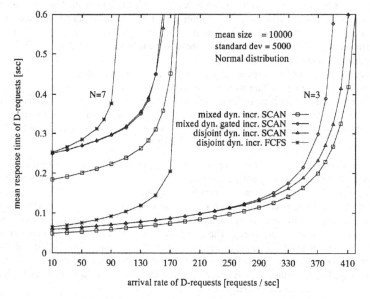

Figure 10.   Mean response time of small D-requests.

Figure 10 shows results for smaller D-request sizes, characterized by the values given in Table 3. As expected, the effect is that the FCFS policy saturates earlier and that both SCAN algorithms can sustain more than twice the load for which the FCFS policy saturates.

In another experiment we increased the coefficient of variation ($Var[S_D]/E[S_D]$) for the values given in Table 2 from 0.5 to 1 by increasing the variance $Var[S_D]$ to $(50000)^2$. The results were practically identical to those shown in figure 9. Using Gamma distributed D-request sizes with the mean value and variance listed in Table 2 also showed no considerable changes.

5.5.   Impact of worst-case assumptions

As described in Section 4, we used a conservative worst-case bound for the rotational latencies in the estimation of the total service time for a disk sweep. A natural question is to what extent this may lead to unutilized disk resources (i.e., idle time within a disk round although the D-request fifo queue is not empty). The alternatives to the worst-case estimation could be the following:

1. Since the rotational latency of a randomly arriving request is uniformly distributed between zero and a full disk revolution, we could derive the probability distribution for the total rotational latency of all requests in the scan list. Then the tail probabilities, e.g., the 99th percentile, of this metric could be used in the estimation of the total service time. This is conservative with high probability (which can be specified as close to 1.0 as one desires) while potentially being more realistic than the conservative worst-case estimation. The desired percentiles can be determined by either explicitly computing the underlying convolution of uniform probability distributions, or by deriving Chernoff bounds from the Laplace-Stieltjes transform [12].

2. We could assume an "omniscient" algorithm that has perfect knowledge about rotational latencies. Such an algorithm would have to keep track of the angular position of the disk head, and it is not clear if this could actually be implemented with sufficient accuracy, without changes to the disk controller which would be beyond our scope anyway. Nevertheless, such an omniscient algorithm can serve as a yardstick against which the suboptimality of the realistic algorithms should be judged.

It turns out, however, that for practical purposes using worst-case bounds for the rotational latency does not cause significant performance penalties. For incremental policies, after each request execution the estimated service time is replaced by the actually needed service time and the scan queue is refilled with requests in scan direction. This happens if the service time has been overestimated. So an estimation at the beginning of a round converts to the exact values during the sweep. The drawback of a non-omniscient algorithm is that requests may be delayed due to the overestimation at the beginning of the round and that these requests cannot be considered later when there is remaining time but the disk head has already passed their position. As shown in figure 11 this does not effect the mean waiting time significantly (parameters of request sizes are listed in Table 3).

5.6. Computational overhead

To estimate the computational overhead of the dynamically incremental scheduling policy we measured the actual execution times for computing the scan list on a UltraSparc machine with 167 Mhz. Without any optimizations of our code, computing all scan lists for a disk in a round takes between 0.8 and 14 milliseconds, depending on the number of requests served per round. Table 4 shows these results fro D-request sizes specified in Table 2. Even

Table 4. Computational overhead per round.

	$N = 7$				
Arrival rate λ [requests/s]	30	60	90	100	110
Overhead [ms]	0.8	1.3	1.9	2.5	3.5
	$N = 3$				
Arrival rate λ [requests/s]	90	150	250	260	270
Overhead [ms]	1	2	6.6	9	13.5

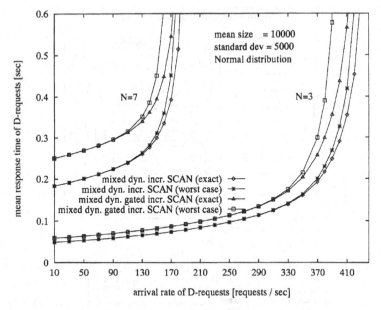

Figure 11.   Impact of worst-case rotational delay.

in the worst case, the computational overhead is only in the order of one percent of the round length. Thus the overhead is rather negligible, especially when taking into account that code optimizations and faster CPUs could presumably speed up the computations of the scheduler by an order of magnitude.

6.   Prototype implementation

The presented scheduling algorithms are being integrated into a full-fledged prototype implementation of a mixed-workload multimedia information system. This system consists of an *Information Server* and *Clients* connected in an intranet environment. The architecture of our prototype is shown in figure 12. The mixed-workload information server itself consists of several components that are briefly described in the following.

(a) *Content manager*: The *Content Manager* stores meta information about the D-data and the C-data. It delivers information about the locations of data on disk to the *Scheduler* and provides a directory of all stored files.
(b) *Scheduler*: The Scheduler implements the algorithms and data structures developed in this paper. For each disk there is a dedicated *Disk Scheduler*. Within each Disk Scheduler two threads run concurrently. The *Generator* thread generates low-level D- and C-requests from client requests by consulting the Content Manager. D-requests are

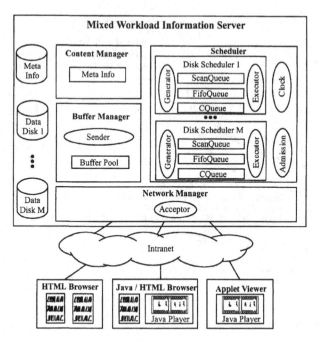

Figure 12. Prototype architecture.

inserted into the *FifoQueue* and the *ScanQueue*, C-requests valid for the next round are inserted into the *CQueue*. The *Executor* thread executes these requests by calling low level I/O functions of the operating system. All data is transferred to a buffer within the *Buffer Pool of* the *Buffer Manager*. To synchronize all threads, the *Clock* thread generates synchronous time events and informs the Scheduler when the current round has expired. The admission control for newly arriving C-requests is performed by the *Admission* thread.

(c) *Buffer manager*: The *Sender* thread within the Buffer Manager transmits data to the clients over the network. It manages a pool of buffers that temporarily store the data read from the disks until the transmission over the network has been completed.

(d) *Network manager*: The *Network Manager* handles connections to the clients. The *Acceptor* thread is responsible for accepting incoming data requests and forwarding these requests to the Scheduler. A subset of the HTTP protocol is supported for retrieving discrete data files. For continuous data, a special purpose protocol has been implemented.

The information server is implemented in C++ using the Standard Template Library (STL) and it is runnning on a multiprocessor Sun Enterprise Server under Sun Solaris 2.5.1.

Since our multimedia information server implements a simple HTTP server, discrete data on the server can be accessed using conventional HTML browsers. For the display of continuous data we use a platform independent Java applet based on the Java Media Framework from Sun. The applet is able to connect to our server and to play continuous videos in streaming mode on Solaris and NT clients. The applet itself is stored as discrete data on the server and downloaded each time it is activated. Using a Java-enabled HTML browser, it is possible to display discrete and continuous data within the same user environment.

7. Conclusion

Our performance results have shown that policies that mix C-requests and D-requests within a scheduling round are superior to approaches that separate service periods for C- and D-requests. Moreover, among these policies the *mixed dynamically incremental SCAN* policy is the clear winner and thus the method of choice for building a mixed-workload multimedia information server. It outperforms all other policies in terms of the D-request response time while still being able to avoid glitches for the C-data streams. In addition, we have shown that such an advanced scheduling policy can be implemented in a reasonably simple manner and has tolerable run-time overhead. Future work may proceed in a number of possible directions:

- It turned out in the performance evaluation that the service time estimation that is needed by the incremental scheduling policy does not depend on perfectly accurate information about disk service parameters, since estimation errors are dynamically corrected as requests are completed. Nevertheless, it could be interesting to further explore the performance potential of more accurate a-priori information. Most notably, one could consider request orderings within a disk sweep other than by cylinder number. Particularly, one could aim to reduce rotational latencies within a sufficiently small range of neighboring cylinders by allowing the request order to deviate from the cylinder-number ordering. Such a more flexible reordering may reduce the total service time at the expense of slightly increased seek times. Limited forms of such optimizations have been implemented in disk controllers [18], but the general optimization problem leads to a computationally expensive travelling salesman problem. Advanced scheduling heuristics based on these considerations are being pursued in [19] (see also [21] for related approaches to disk scheduling in general).
- A degree of freedom in our framework of scheduling policies that we have not further pursued in this paper is the number of subrounds per round. Tuning round and subround lengths is an issue that deserves further investigation. Recent work along these lines has been reported in [8]. In contrast to the incremental mixed-period scheduling policy developed in this paper, introducing subrounds needs to consider the risk of glitches in C-data streams much more carefully, and this is why we disregarded this family of policies in the current paper.
- Finally, the most challenging research avenue for future work is to develop analytical underpinnings for predicting the performance of incremental scheduling algorithms, given the various workload parameters. We plan to continue our earlier work on server configuration [15, 16] by replacing the previously used simple two-period scheduling policy with the much more elaborated mixed scheduling policy developed in the current paper. An accurate, analytical performance prediction is needed as the basis for a system

configuration tool that should serve two purposes: 1) determining the hardware resources needed for a multimedia server with a given workload and specified service quality goals, and 2) dynamically adjusting admission control and load management parameters at run-time. Work along these lines is of high practical relevance as it allows a service provider to offer multimedia server facilities with guaranteed service quality at minimal cost, making the best use of the available resources, also in case of dynamically evolving workloads.

Acknowledgments

This work has been supported by the ESPRIT Long Term Research Project HERMES.

References

1. S. Berson, S. Ghandeharizadeh, and R. Muntz, "Staggered striping in multimedia information systems," in Proceedings ACM SIGMOD Conference 1994, International Conference on Management of Data, Minneapolis, Minnesota, May 1994, pp. 79–90.
2. E. Chang and A. Zakhor, "Cost analyses for VBR video servers," in Proceedings of IS&T/SPIE International Symposium on Electronic Imaging: Science and Technology, San Jose, California, January 1996.
3. M.-S. Chen, D.D. Kandlur, and P.S. Yu, "Optimization of the grouped sweeping scheduling (GSS) with heterogenous multimedia streams," in Proceedings of the ACM International Conference on Multimedia, ACM Multimedia '93, Anaheim, CA, 1993.
4. R. Geist and S. Daniel, "A continuum of disk scheduling algorithms," ACM Transactions on Computer Systems, Vol. 5, No. 1, pp. 77–92, 1987.
5. D.J. Gemmel, J. Han, R. Beaton, and S. Christodoulakis, "Delay-sensitive multimedia on disks," IEEE Multimedia, pp. 57–67, 1995.
6. D.J. Gemmel, H.M. Vin, D.D. Kandlur, P.V. Rangan, and L.A. Rowe, "Multimedia storage servers: A tutorial," IEEE Computer, pp. 40–49, 1995.
7. S. Ghandeharizadeh, S.H. Kim, and C. Shahabi, "On disk scheduling and data placement for video servers," ACM Multimedia Systems, 1996.
8. L. Golubchik, J.C.S. Lui, E. de Silva e Souza, and H.R. Gail, "Evaluation of tradeoffs in resource management techniques for multimedia storage servers," Technical Report CS-TR# 3904, Department of Computer Science, University of Maryland, 1998.
9. S. Hollfelder, A. Kraiss, and T. Rakow, "A client-controlled adaptation framework for multimedia database systems," in Proceedings European Workshop on Interactive Distributed Multimedia Systems and Telecommunications Services, Darmstadt, Germany, 1997.
10. C. Martin, P.S. Narayan, B. Özden, R. Rastogi, and A. Silberschatz, "The Fellini multimedia storage server," in Multimedia Information Storage and Management, Soon M. Chung (Ed.), Kluwer, 1996.
11. Mesquite Software, Inc., CSIM18 simulation engine: User's guide, http://www.mesquite.com.
12. R. Nelson, Probability, Stochastic Processes, and Queueing Theory: The Mathematics of Computer Performance Modeling, Springer, 1995.
13. G. Nerjes, P. Muth, M. Paterakis, Y. Romboyannakis, P. Triantafillou, and G. Weikum, "Scheduling strategies for mixed workloads in multimedia information servers," in Proceedings IEEE International Workshop on Research Issues in Data Engineering (RIDE'98), Orlando, Florida, 1998.
14. G. Nerjes, P. Muth, and G. Weikum, "Stochastic service guarantees for continuous data on multi-zone disks," in Proceedings ACM Symposium on Principles of Database Systems (PODS), Tucson, Arizona, 1997.
15. G. Nerjes, P. Muth, and G. Weikum, "Stochastic performance guarantees for mixed workloads in a multimedia information system," in Proceedings IEEE International Workshop on Research Issues in Data Engineering (RIDE'97), Birmingham, UK, 1997.
16. G. Nerjes, Y. Romboyannakis, P. Muth, M. Paterakis, P. Triantafillou, and G. Weikum, "On mixed-workload multimedia storage servers with guaranteed performance and service quality," in Proceedings 3rd International Workshop on Multimedia Information Systems, Como, Italy, 1997.

17. B. Özden, R. Rastogi, and A. Silberschatz, "Disk striping in video server environments," in Proceedings IEEE International Conference on Multimedia Computing and Systems, June 1996.
18. Quantum Corporation, "ORCA: A new command reordering technique," http://www.quantum.com/src/ storage_basics.
19. Y. Romboyannakis, G. Nerjes, P. Muth, M. Paterakis, P. Triantafillou, and G. Weikum, "Disk scheduling for mixed-media workload in a multimedia server," in Proceedings of the 6th ACM International Conference on Multimedia, Bristol, U.K., 1998.
20. C. Ruemmler and J. Wilkes, "An introduction to disk drive modelling," IEEE Computer, pp. 17–28, 1994.
21. B. Seeger, "An analysis of schedules for performing multi-page requests," Informations Systems, Vol. 21, No. 5, pp. 387–407, 1996.
22. A. Silberschatz and P. Galvin, Operating System Concepts, 4th edition, Addison-Wesley: New York, 1994.
23. P. Shenoy and H.M. Vin, "Cello: A disk scheduling framework for next generation operating systems," in Proceedings ACM SIGMETRICS Conference, June 1998.
24. H. Thimm, W. Klas, C. Cowan, J. Walpole, and C. Pu, "Optimization of adaptive data-flows for competing multimedia presentational database sessions," in Proceedings IEEE International Conference on Multimedia Computing and Systems, Ottawa, Canada, 1997.
25. F.A. Tobagi, J. Pang, R. Baird, and M. Gang, "Streaming RAID—A disk array management system for video files," ACM Multimedia Conference, 1993.
26. P. Triantafillou and C. Faloutsos, "Overlay striping for optimal parallel I/O in modern applications," Parallel Computing Journal, Vol. 41, No. 1, pp. 21–43, 1998.
27. H.M. Vin, P. Goyal, A. Goyal, and A. Goyal, "A statistical admission control algorithm for multimedia servers," ACM Multimedia Conference, 1994.
28. B.L. Worthington, G.R. Ganger, and Y.N. Patt, "Scheduling algorithms for modern disk drives," in Proceedings ACM SIGMETRICS Conference, 1994.

Guido Nerjes received his diploma degree (Dipl.-Inform.) from the Technical University of Braunschweig, Germany, in 1996. From 1996 to 1998 he was affiliated with the Institute of Information Systems at ETH Zurich where he was involved in the Esprit research project Hermes. He is currently finishing his doctoral thesis at the Computer Science Department at the University of the Saarland. His research interests include analytic performance modeling and evaluation of multimedia information and database systems.

Peter Muth received the diploma degree (Dipl.-Inform.) and the doctoral degree (Dr.-Ing.) both in computer science from the University of Darmstadt, Germany, in 1989 and 1994, respectively. He is currently affiliated with an insurance company, Berlinische Leben AG in Wiesbaden. Until 1994 he was leading a department in the Integrated Publication and Information Systems Institute (IPSI) of the National Research Center for Information Technology (GMD) in Darmstadt. From 1994 to 1998 he was an Assistant Professor in the Department of Computer Science of the University of the Saarland at Saarbruecken, Germany. Dr. Muth's research interests include parallel and distributed information systems, multimedia information systems and workflow management.

Michael Paterakis received his Diploma degree from the National Technical University of Athens. Greece, his M.Sc. degree from the University of Connecticut, and his Ph.D. degree from the University of Virginia, in 1984, 1986, and 1988, respectively, all in Electrical Engineering. Since 1995, he is an Associate Professor in the Department of Electronic and Computer Engineering at the Technical University of Crete, Greece. He was an Associate Professor in the Department of Computer and Information Sciences at the University of Delaware, where he has been since September 1988. During the summer of 1991, he was a Visiting Professor in the Department of Electronic and Computer Engineering, Technical University of Crete, Greece. His research interests include computer communication networks with emphasis on protocol design, modeling and performance evaluation of broadband high speed multimedia networks, multiple access wireless communication systems, and of packet radio networks; centralized and distributed multimedia information delivery systems; queueing and applied probability theory and their application to communication networks and computer systems. He has published more than 60 technical papers in archival journals, refereed conference proceedings and edited books, in the abovementioned technical areas. He served on the Technical Program Committees of the 1991 International Conference on Distributed Computing Systems, the 1992 and 1994 IEEE INFOCOM Conferences, the 1997 IEEE Workshop on the Architecture and Implementation of High Performance Communication Subsystems (HPCS'97), and the 1998 IFIP Workshop on Performance Modeling and Evaluation of ATM Networks. He has reviewed extensively for all of the major archival journals (published by IEEE, ACM, IEE, and Elsevier Publ.), and IEEE sponsored international conferences in his areas of expertise. Professor Paterakis is a Senior Member of the IEEE. He is also a member of the IEEE Technical Committees on Computer Communications and on the Internet, the Greek Chamber of Professional Engineers, and the Greek Association of Electrical and Electronic Engineers.

Yannis Romboyannakis was born in Heraklion, Crete, Greece, in 1973. He received his Diploma degree in Electronics and Computer Engineering from the Technical University of Crete, Greece, in 1996, where he also received his M.Sc. degree in 1998. He is currently a Ph.D. candidate in the Production and Management Engineering Department of the Technical University of Crete. His research interests focus on the design and performance evaluation of computer communication and multimedia information systems, queueing and applied probability theory and their application to computer communication and information systems and Web Commerce Technology.

Peter Triantafillou was born in Toronto Canada in 1963. He received the Ph.D. degree from the Department of Computer Science, at the University of Waterloo, Waterloo, Canada in 1991. From September 1991 till August 1996 he was an Assistant Professor at the School of Computing Science at Simon Fraser University, Vancouver, Canada. From September 1994 till January 1996 he was on a leave of absence at the Technical University of Crete, Greece. Since January 1996, he has been with the Department of Electronic and Computer Engineering at the Technical University of Crete, Greece. Currently, Prof. Triantafillou's research focuses in the area of high-performance, intelligent storage systems, including disk drives, disk arrays, and robotic tape/disk libraries, with a special emphasis on multimedia applications. His research activities in the past have focused on multidatabases, distributed file systems, and highly-available distributed databases. Prof. Triantafillou has served in the Program Committees of the ACM MobiDE '99, ACM SIGMOD '99, FODO '98, RIDE '98, and EDBT '98 international conferences and as a reviewer in most relevant international journals.

Gerhard Weikum received the diploma degree (Dipl.-Inform.) and the doctoral degree (Dr.-Ing.) both in computer science from the University of Darmstadt, Germany, in 1982 and 1986, respectively. Dr Weikum is a Full Professor in the Department of Computer Science of the University of the Saarland at Saarbruecken, Germany, where he is leading a research group on database systems. His former affiliations include MCC at Austin, Texas, and ETH Zurich in Switzerland. During his sabbatical in 1997, he was a visiting Senior Researcher in the database research group of Microsoft. Dr. Weikum's research interests include parallel and distributed information systems, transaction processing and workflow management, and database optimization and performance evaluation. Dr. Weikum serves on the editorial boards of ACM Transactions on Database Systems, The VLDB Journal, and the Distributed and Parallel Databases Journal. He has served on numerous program committees of international conferences, he was the program committee co-chair of the 4th International Conference on Parallel and Distributed Information Systems, and he is the program committee co-chair of the 16th IEEE International Conference on Data Engineering. Dr. Weikum has been elected onto the board of trustees of the VLDB Endowment.

Threshold-Based Dynamic Replication in Large-Scale Video-on-Demand Systems

PETER W.K. LIE AND JOHN C.S. LUI
Department of Computer Science & Engineering, The Chinese University of Hong Kong, Hong Kong

LEANA GOLUBCHIK
Department of Computer Science and UMIACS, University of Maryland, College Park, MD, 20742

Abstract. Recent advances in high speed networking technologies and video compression techniques have made Video-on-Demand (VOD) services feasible. A large-scale VOD system imposes a large demand on I/O bandwidth and storage resources, and therefore, parallel disks are typically used for providing VOD service. Although striping of movie data across a large number of disks can balance the utilization among these disks, such a striping technique can exhibit additional complexity, for instance, in data management, such as synchronization among disks during data delivery, as well as in supporting fault tolerant behavior. Therefore, it is more practical to limit the extent of data striping, for example, by arranging the disks in groups (or nodes) and then allowing intra-group (or intra-node) data striping only. With multiple striping groups, however, we may need to assign a movie to multiple nodes so as to satisfy the total demand of requests for that movie. Such an approach gives rise to several design issues, including: (1) what is the right number of copies of each movie we need so as to satisfy the demand and at the same time not waste storage capacity, (2) how to assign these movies to different nodes in the system, and (3) what are efficient approaches to altering the number of copies of each movie (and their placement) when the need for that arises. In this paper, we study an approach to dynamically reconfiguring the VOD system so as to alter the number of copies of each movie maintained on the server as the access demand for these movies fluctuates. We propose various approaches to addressing the above stated issues, which result in a VOD design that is adaptive to the changes in data access patterns. Performance evaluation is carried out to quantify the costs and the performance gains of these techniques.

Keywords: Video-on-Demand, storage systems, dynamic replication, large-scale systems, multimedia

1. Introduction

Recent technological advances in information and communication technologies have made multimedia on-demand services, such as movies-on-demand, home-shopping, etc., feasible. Due to the enormous storage and bandwidth requirements of multimedia data, such systems are expected to have very large disk farms. Thus, it would be unrealistic to consider a centralized design of a video server, using a single disk cluster and/or a single processing node. A more viable architecture would be a parallel system with multiple processing nodes in which each node has its own collection of disks and these nodes are interconnected, e.g., via a high-speed switch such as an ATM switch.

One difficulty in designing a large parallel information system is the choice of data placement techniques. The distribution of data among the nodes of the system can significantly affect the overall performance of that system—inappropriate data distribution can lead to load imbalance problems due to skewness in the data access patterns. In a large parallel VOD system improper data distribution can lead to a situation where requests for (popular) objects can not be serviced even when the overall capacity of the system is not exhausted because these objects reside on highly loaded nodes, i.e., the available capacity and the necessary data are not on the same node.

One approach to addressing the load imbalance problem is to stripe each object across all the nodes/disks in the system and thus avoid the problem of "splitting resources", e.g., as in the staggered striping technique [1]. However, this approach suffers from the following shortcomings. A processing node can only be attached to a limited number of disks, therefore, a multi-node system must be considered which results in additional complexity, e.g., some form of synchronization in delivery of a single object from multiple nodes would have to be addressed. In addition, it is not practical to assume that a system can be constructed from homogeneous disks, i.e., as the system grows[1] we would be forced to use disks with different transfer and storage capacity characteristics—having to stripe objects across heterogeneous disks would lead to further complications. Finally, an increase in the size of the disk subsystem will result in (potential) "re-striping" of all objects.

Another approach to addressing skews in data access is replication of popular objects [3, 11]. That is, instead of striping each object across all the nodes, we can replicate the popular objects on several nodes in hopes of providing sufficient bandwidth capacity to service the demand for these objects. The difficulty here is deciding: (a) how many copies of each object to keep, which can be determined by the demand for that movie, e.g., as in [11], and (b) on which node to keep each copy, which should be done in such a manner as to spread the (anticipated) load as evenly as possible among the nodes (adjustments to load imbalance can be made during system operation as in [11]). Inappropriate choices in resolving these issues can lead to poor resource utilization.

In order to achieve better resource utilization characteristics, the number of replicas of each object should change over time, as the object access patterns change. One approach to dealing with this problem is to periodically adjust the number of copies, e.g., as in [11]. Another approach to dealing with changes in access patterns is to replicate objects *dynamically*, as demand for it arises, where the objective is to perform the replication efficiently and in such a manner as to reduce the probability of request rejection. This dynamic approach is motivated by the fact that such a system should be more responsive to changes in the workload and thus result in better performance. *Dynamic replication* of objects in parallel VOD systems is the focus of our work in this paper.

Clearly, dynamic replication is only useful if it can be performed reasonably fast so as to result in some benefit. Furthermore, since dynamic replication could result in significant system overheads, e.g., in the form of additional I/O disk retrievals, memory buffers, and communication bandwidth, in designing such a system, we must also address the following questions: (1) what are efficient replication algorithms for video data which do not incur significant system overheads and (2) what are appropriate trigger mechanisms for initiating replication or deletion of a video object—a poor choice of triggers can cause the system to perform unnecessary replication or deletion which can lead to a waste of system resources, e.g., if a deleted object is replicated in the "near" future. Specifically, we will investigate *threshold-based* trigger methods. As already mentioned, the cost of altering the number of replicas is significant, and the use of a threshold-based approach can result in a cost-controlled creation and deletion of these replicas [6], according to the changes in the access patterns.

Thus, in this paper we will study the following issues: (1) how to perform movie replication in a manner that reduces the replication time—the tradeoff that needs to be considered here is between dedicating more system resources for replication in order to put a new replica into service *earlier* (in hopes of being able to satisfy more requests once the replica is in place) versus dedicating these resources for normal processing of arriving requests, (2) when are the appropriate times to replicate and de-replicate (remove a replica of) a movie, and (3) how to choose a movie and the nodes for replication and de-replication. We investigate several policies for each of these issues and carry out performance studies to quantify the associated performance gains, which include: (1) assessment of replication time and (2) evaluation of the tradeoff between using resources for reducing movie replication time or using these resources for servicing normal movie requests.

Related works on replication of movies (in addition to the ones already mentioned above) include the following. In [9], the authors evaluated the use of redundancy schemes for cost-effective data placement in disk arrays for VOD servers. In [4, 5, 10, 11], the authors also consider dynamic replication as an approach to dealing with load imbalance. The work presented in this paper differs in several aspects, including the consideration of available capacity and the use of a threshold-based approach to trigger replication as well as in focusing on the replication policies themselves and the exhibition of the tradeoffs associated with such policies.

2. System model

In this section, we describe the model of our VOD system.[2] Let $S = \{n_1, n_2, \ldots, n_N\}$ where n_i represents the ith node of the system. All nodes in the VOD system are connected, e.g., by a high-speed interconnect switch (such as an ATM switch, a cross-bar switch, etc.). Note that a node is a high-level abstraction of a storage subsystem, which is likely to be a collection of physically attached storage devices (like a disk array) together with server hardware (if the storage subsystem is not a *network attached peripheral*, i.e., a stand alone storage device connected to the network for the sole purpose of providing disk access to other servers). Therefore, in our paper, a node is a generalization of a *disk striping group* and a *logical disk* in [11] and [5], respectively.

Each node $x \in S$ has a finite storage capacity, and a finite service capacity B_x (usually limited by the bandwidth resources, performance characteristics of storage media, server processing power, etc.), which is measured in units of movie-access streams. This model allows the nodes to be heterogeneous in terms of both storage and service capacities. Since in this paper we discuss disk-based replication techniques, we do not require the presence of tertiary storage, such as a tape library, for the use of our techniques. However, if a tape library is present, it can be treated as a special node that has very low service capacity, solely for providing movie data and does not directly provide VOD service, unlike other nodes.

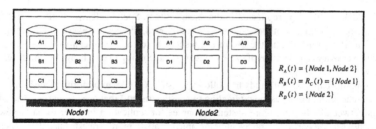

Figure 1. Example of a VOD system with two nodes ($|S| = 2$).

The load on node x at time t is denoted by $L_x(t)$, again in units of movie-access streams. Multiple copies of the same movie i may be stored on different nodes known as *replica nodes*. The set of these nodes is denoted by $R_i(t) \subseteq S$. Note that $R_i(t)$ is a function of time since in our VOD system, we are using dynamic replication and the number of copies of a movie may vary with changes in its popularity. Figure 1 shows a system with two nodes and four movies. There are two copies of movie A, each stored on one of the nodes. There is only one copy of movies B, C, and D. Each copy of a movie is striped across the three disks of a node.[3]

Customers arrive to the VOD system at an average rate of λ. Upon a customer arrival at time t, there is a probability of $p_i(t)$ that movie i is requested. The admission policy then examines the load of each node in the set $R_i(t)$. If sufficient capacity for servicing the new request is available on at least one of the nodes in $R_i(t)$, then the customer request is accepted by the system and assigned to the least-loaded node in $R_i(t)$. Otherwise the customer is rejected.[4]

For ease of reference, the following table summarizes all the notation used in this paper. Some of the notation given in the table will be defined later in the paper, as it is needed.

S	set of all nodes in the system
N	number of nodes, which is equal to $|S|$
m_i	length of movie i (in minutes)
λ	average request arrival rate to the VOD system
B_x	maximum service capacity of node x (in streams)
$L_x(t)$	load on node x at time t (in streams)
$A_i(t)$	*available service capacity* of movie i at time t (in streams)
$R_i(t)$	set of replica nodes for movie i at time t
n_s	source node for replication
n_t	target node for replication
$T_i(t)$	*replication threshold* of movie i at time t
$p_i(t)$	probability that an arriving customer at time t chooses movie i for viewing
ϕ	hard limit of replication streams
h	*threshold limit* parameter to control replication

3. Replication methodology

In general, replication of a movie i involves copying of movie i from a *source node* $n_s \in R_i(t)$ to a *target node* $n_t \notin R_i(t)$. There are a number of issues involved in such a dynamic replication of movies. These issues include:[5] 1) when should replication be invoked, 2) how to select a source node and a target node for replication, 3) how should replication be performed and 4) when and how should *de-replication* (removal of a replica) of a movie be done.

Note that some of these issues are analogous to those in the field of processor load balancing [2], but in a more complicated form. Generally speaking, in the processor load balancing problem, a task can be executed by any node (perhaps at different costs). In VOD systems, however, there is an additional level of complexity. This is due to the fact that only a subset of nodes can serve requests for a movie (i.e., a request for movie i can only be serviced by the nodes in $R_i(t)$). Dynamic replication allows this subset to be changed continually, if such a need arises due to the demand for that movie.

3.1. Replication triggering policy

We adopt a threshold-based policy for triggering movie replication. The main motivation for using a threshold-based approach is that there is a non-negligible cost for creating or removing a replica. And, as in most practical situations, an important concern is not only the system performance but rather its cost/performance ratio. More specifically, under "light" loads, it is not desirable to create a movie replica unless there is a sufficient demand that would justify the cost of its creation; on the other hand, it is also not desirable for a system to exhibit poor performance (e.g., a high request rejection rate), which can result due to lack of replicas under "heavy" loads. One approach to improving the cost/performance ratio of a system is to react to changes in workload through the use of threshold-based policies.

For the following discussion, we define the *available service capacity* for movie i at time t, $A_i(t)$, to be:

$$A_i(t) = \sum_{x \in R_i(t)} (B_x - L_x(t)) \tag{1}$$

We will use the notion of available service capacity in defining a threshold-based replication triggering policy.

The aim of replication is to allow more nodes to handle requests for viewing a particular movie when necessary, thereby decreasing the number of customer rejections. Therefore, when the available service capacity $A_i(t)$ for movie i offered by its replica nodes $R_i(t)$ is too low, it is time to create an additional copy of that movie. Thus we define the following policy for triggering replication.

When a customer request arrives for movie i at time t, replication of movie i is to be initiated if and only if all of the following criteria are met:

- $A_i(t) < T_i(t)$, where $T_i(t)$ is a *threshold* parameter in our replication algorithm. In our study, we use a heuristic setting of $T_i(t) = \min(p_i(t)\lambda m_i, h\bar{B})$ in which $p_i(t)\lambda$ is an estimate of the average arrival rate for request of movie i and $\bar{B}$ is the mean service capacity of a node. The rationale behind the use of $p_i(t)\lambda m_i$ in the evaluation function is that we need at most m_i amount of time[6] to replicate a movie to gain additional service capacity for movie i. If replication of movie i is invoked at time t when $A_i(t) < p_i(t)\lambda m_i$, the expected number of arrivals during the movie replication time, the system may have to reject some customers before movie i is completely replicated.[7] Therefore, to avoid rejecting customer, the system initiates the movie replication at this threshold. The *threshold limit* parameter h is introduced to control excessive replication of very popular movies. The impact of the parameter h will be illustrated in Section 4.

- The system is not currently replicating movie i, i.e., at any time t there will not be more than one replication process going on for movie i.
- There are suitable nodes and enough resources that satisfy the requirements of the nodes selection and replication policies, to be described in the Sections 3.2 & 3.3 respectively.

When the VOD system decides to initiate the movie replication process, the next issue to be addressed is the choice of an appropriate source node n_s and a target node n_t. This issue is addressed in the following section.

3.2. Source & target nodes selection policies

To replicate a movie i in the VOD system, we choose a node from the following set S_s of *least-loaded* nodes (relative to their full service capacities):

$$S_s = \left\{ x \mid \text{where } L_x(t) = \max_{y \in R_i(t)} \{B_y - L_y(t)\} \right\} \tag{2}$$

The rationale for choosing a least-loaded node is that some of the replication policies (to be described in the next section) may result in an additional load on the source node n_s. Thus to reduce the probability of replication interfering with the normal workload (i.e., with future requests for movies), we choose the least loaded of the possible source nodes in $R_i(t)$.

The target node selection policy is a bit more complicated. A target node n_t should be a *lightly-loaded* one, otherwise there might be little additional service capacity to be gained for a movie after it has been replicated. In our study, we choose a target node from the following set S_t:

$$S_t = \left\{ x \mid \text{where } x \notin R_i(t) \text{ and } L_x(t) < \frac{B_x}{2} \right\} \tag{3}$$

Three target node selection policies are studied in this paper. All of them choose a node from the set of lightly-loaded nodes which do not contain a copy of the movie being replicated:

(1) Randomly choose a node from the set S_t.
(2) Choose the *least-loaded* node. Mathematically, we choose the node from the set S_t^1 where

$$S_t^1 = \left\{ x \mid \text{where } x \in S_t \text{ and } L_x(t) = \max_{y \in S_t} \{B_y - L_y(t)\} \right\} \tag{4}$$

Note that this policy suffers from a problem of *competition for service capacity* by multiple movies. This problem arises when there are are several movie replication processes going on at the same time, and all these processes are trying to write to the same target node. When these processes are completed, the remaining service capacity at that node will be shared among several movies, which are all in need of more service capacity.

(3) Choose one which has the highest *estimated residual capacity*. Mathematically, we choose the node from the set S_t^2 where

$$S_t^2 = \left\{ x \mid \text{where } x \in S_t \text{ and } L_x(t) = \max_{y \in S_t} \left\{ \frac{B_y - L_y(t)}{1 + \gamma_y(t)} \right\} \right\} \tag{5}$$

and $\gamma_x(t)$ is the number of movies being replicated to node x at time t. Since the residual service capacity is divided by $1 + \gamma_x(t)$, this policy avoids simultaneous replication of different movies to the same target node. Therefore, it reduces the likelihood of competition for service capacity, as described above.

3.3. Replication policies

The basic mechanism for performing movie replication is to use the residual service capacity of a node—that is, we *inject* an additional reading stream on a source node n_s and a writing stream on a target node n_t so as to replicate the movie. However, there are other more *efficient* ways to replicate a movie. For example, consider the case where the replication of movie i is triggered by a customer arrival for movie i only; then, the resources allocated for servicing that arriving customer request can be used for replication as well by multicasting read data to the customer and to the target replication node, i.e., we can *piggyback* [7] upon a customer which is currently viewing the movie we want to replicate. Note that, this piggybacking technique does not require injection of an additional (reading) stream at the source node n_s, and thus replication through piggybacking does not create an additional load at the source node.

Replication of a movie through piggybacking or injection of a single stream at the source node, termed as *sequential replication*, can take on the order of 1–2 hours (i.e., the duration of the movie, m_i). Another approach to improving the performance of the system is to reduce the movie replication time. With shorter replication times, movie replicas are available sooner to serve customer requests, leading to a reduction in the customer rejection rate. Based on this concept, let us consider some *parallel replication* strategies—strategies which utilize multiple concurrent streams for replicating different partitions of the same movie so as to shorten the replication time. For example, if the system can support four additional streams at both the source node n_s and the target node n_t as in figure 4, a 120-minute movie can be replicated by injecting four concurrent streams for replicating four different 30-minute partitions of the movie, reducing the replication time to 30 minutes.

Although running sequential replication at r times the normal speed yields replication times similar to those achieved by parallel replication with r streams, one of the advantages parallel replication provides over a high-speed sequential replication is that it avoids the problem that increased access speeds may affect disk scheduling. Usually, scheduling of concurrent stream access to movies stored on a disk array depend on the access speed needed to satisfy the real-time constraints of delivery of the movie data. When the access speed of a movie is changed, it may disrupt the scheduling of other movies being accessed on the same disk array. Of course, the scheduling algorithm may be changed to cope with such high-speed replication streams, but such changes may result in additional costs.

3.3.1. Policy 1: Injected sequential replication. This is the basic replication policy in which a reading stream is injected into the node n_s and a writing stream is injected into the node n_t. The reading stream will read the movie from the beginning to the end in a sequential fashion and at the rate of a normal viewing customer. Any data read by the reading stream is then forwarded to the writing stream in the target node. In this replication policy, the replication time is simply the length of the movie i, m_i.

Assuming the customers playback movies sequentially from the beginning to the end, it is possible to direct new arrivals for a movie, which is being replicated, to the target node, even if the replication has not been completed yet. This is because the replication process has been started from the beginning of the movie, and both the replication and the playback proceed at the same rate. By the time the customer needs to read a block of movie data, the block would have already been replicated under the sequential viewing assumption. We call this *early acceptance* by the target node. With early acceptance, the system can make use of a replica quickly.

Note that early acceptance technique possesses a drawback. This is because most of the time early accepted customers would be viewing incomplete copies of movies, so no fast forward beyond the replicated partition is possible for them. We call the position beyond which no fast forward can be made a *fast forward limit*. Figure 2 shows two early accepted

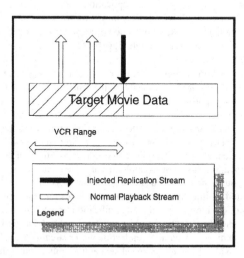

Figure 2.   Early acceptance.

customers viewing an incomplete copy of a movie, which is being written to the storage sub-system by an injected replication stream. It can be seen from the figure that the two early accepted customers cannot fast forward to the second half of the movie, because that part has not been written to the storage yet. This fast forward limit is time-varying because the replication process will continue until it is completed. A solution to this problem is to migrate the customer, who has issued a fast forward request, to another node which has a complete copy of the movie. If no other node can serve it, the fast forward request has to be rejected or delayed. If rejection of VCR requests is unacceptable, this early acceptance technique should not be adopted.

3.3.2. Policy 2: Piggybacked sequential replication.

By using the *piggybacking technique* [7] and exploiting the sequential pattern of movie viewing, movie data can be read from the source node n_s without injecting an additional reading stream on the node n_s. With this policy, the replication process piggybacks upon the viewing customer who has triggered the replication, i.e., when some movie data is read, the system will multicast the data to the viewing customer and at the same time, to the target node n_t. Figure 3 shows four customers viewing a movie, one of which has been chosen for piggybacked replication of that movie to the target node.

Note that using the piggybacking technique, the system does encountered one drawback. In this case, if the piggybacked customer performs any VCR function (pause, fast forward or rewind), the replication will be affected. For example, if the customer performs a pause or a rewind operation, the replication has to be paused, until the customer resumes normal playback. If the customer performs a fast forward operation, we may setup the target node to switch to a fast writing mode, provided that the target node has enough residual service

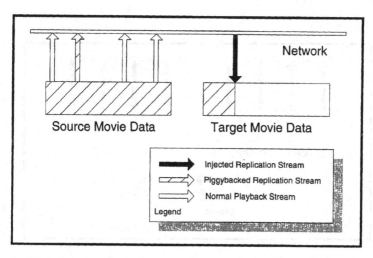

Figure 3. Piggybacked sequential replication.

capacity for this. In this case, the replication will be done sooner than in the normal case. If the target node does not possess enough service capacity for replication in a fast forward mode, or the customer stops viewing the movie, a way to deal with such situation is to replace the piggybacking operation by injecting a replication stream, i.e., the replication process changes from the piggybacked mode to the injected mode. This fallback-based solution may also be employed in the case of occurrence of other types of VCR functions that may act on a piggybacked playback stream. In case the source node runs out of service capacity and thus cannot perform the fallback, the system may wait for a certain period for service capacity to be released by other streams before canceling the replication.

This drawback of piggybacking causes another problem with early acceptance. In the event that the system is waiting for service capacity availability, or the replication has been canceled, then if there are some early accepted customers at the target node, the customers may reach the end of the incomplete copy of the movie being replicated. Beyond this point no movie data is available to continue the movie playback. Although migrating the customers to other nodes would allow the continuation of the movie playback, migration causes additional complexities, and cannot be done when all replica nodes of the movie run out of service capacity.

3.3.3. Policy 3: Injected parallel replication.   The motivation behind the *parallel replication* technique is that by using multiple, equally spaced (in movie time) streams to replicate a movie, the replication time can be reduced significantly. In figure 4, there are four pairs of injected replication streams for the reading and writing of movie data, along with three customers viewing the movie at the source node. Since these four replication streams perform the copying process concurrently, it only takes one-fourth of the movie duration time to complete the replication.

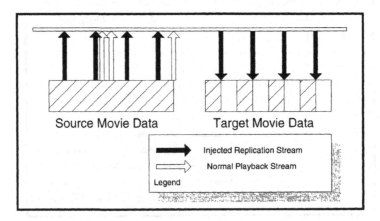

Figure 4.   Injected parallel replication.

If both n_s and n_t can support r additional streams where

$$r = \min\left(B_{n_s} - L_{n_s}(t),\ B_{n_t} - L_{n_t}(t),\ \phi\right) \tag{6}$$

then we can use these r streams to perform parallel replication where movie data is split into r equal partitions, and the corresponding r streams are injected on both nodes, with each stream responsible for one of the partitions. The parameter ϕ is a hard limit on the number of replication streams, which allows the system designer to balance the tradeoff between using more resources to shorten the replication time and leaving more resources for servicing customers in the near future.[8] Note that when $\phi = 1$, this policy becomes a sequential policy. The r added streams represent overhead on both nodes, and by the time m_i/r all streams would have completed their replication for movie i simultaneously.

With multiple replicas of the same movie on the system, it is possible to perform *load balancing* by migrating customers from one replica to another. The subject of how to best utilize a set of nodes for migration to achieve load balance is discussed in [11]. Here we consider the special load balancing technique which we call *early migration*, i.e., migration of customers to replicas that have not been completely replicated. The advantage of employing this aggressive migration technique is that the high level of load associated with a popular movie can be redistributed, if desired for load balancing, to a lightly loaded node very soon after replication has begun. Early migration imposes some restrictions on when the migration can take place, because only certain parts of the movie are present at the target node before the replication is completed. The only times when such migration is possible when customers viewing the movie at the source node reach the replication partition boundaries. They can then be migrated to the target node to continue the movie playback, because the beginning of the succeeding partition has already been replicated. In this manner, many of the existing viewers can be migrated to the replica node, thus quickly reducing the load on the source node if desired.

Early migration is a generalization of early acceptance, thus it suffers from similar problems that affect early acceptance. Recall that early accepted customer will cause problems if they try to issue VCR functions. Likewise, early migrated customers would face similar problems as well. In early migration, the problems are more severe, because early migrated customers would not only see a fast forward limit, but also a *rewind limit* as well. This limit is the beginning boundary of the replication partition which they are currently viewing at the target node, because the ending part of the preceding partition is not available until all the streams have completed their replication. This situation is depicted in figure 5, in which there is an early accepted customer number 1, and an early migrated customer number 2, while two replication streams are carrying out parallel replication using two parallel streams. Customer number 1 faces the fast forward limit. Customer number 2 faces both the fast forward limit and the rewind limit. An approach to addressing this problem is described earlier under the discussion on early acceptance policy.

3.3.4. Policy 4: Piggybacked parallel replication. By applying the piggybacking strategy to parallel replication, reading of the movie data can be accomplished without injecting replication streams on the source node n_s. Under this policy, a number of existing customers

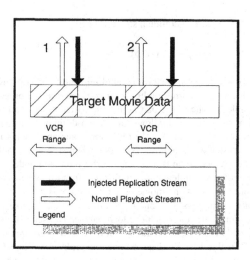

viewing the movie to be replicated are picked for piggybacking. Unlike under the previous policy, it would be difficult to have a simple sequential replication process speed-up to achieve the same level of performance as parallel replication. The chosen set of customers are responsible for piggybacked reading of movie data from their current positions to the initial position of the succeeding viewing customer (or the end of the movie for the final piggybacked viewing customer). This set of customers must include the one that has triggered the replication process, for replication of the beginning part of the movie. In figure 6, there are six customers viewing a movie at the source node, three of which have been chosen for piggybacked replication. Note that the piggybacked customers' distribution is much less uniform than the injected streams in the previous policy (refer to figure 4).

Thus, one issue that needs to be addressed in the piggybacked parallel replication is the proper selection of customers to be used for piggybacking. Since the duration needed to complete replication of the whole movie is dominated by the piggybacked customer who is responsible for the largest part, ideally, if the customers are spread out evenly at different positions of the movie, then the movie replication time will be minimized. Therefore, in selecting the viewing customer for piggybacking, the system tries to emulate the "regular" splitting strategy as used in the previous policy, i.e., all streams replicate the same amount of the movie's data and complete the replication at the same time. In the worst case, the customer which triggered the replication would be at the beginning, but all the remaining customers would be near the end of the movie. Thus one piggybacked stream would be responsible for nearly the whole movie, and other streams would be responsible for negligible small parts only. This is the worst scenario because even if there is extra service capacity in both the source node and target node, effectively there is only one replication stream, i.e., essentially degenerating to a sequential replication process.

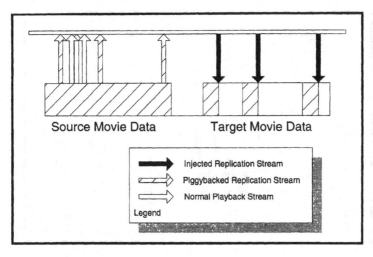

Figure 6. Piggybacked parallel replication.

Since the replication time is determined by the longest partition that needs to be replicated by one stream, the customers should be chosen in such a way as to be as evenly spaced out as possible, yielding partitions of similar lengths. On the other hand, it is clear that the system needs to select the piggybacking customers as fast as possible, otherwise, the VOD service would be affected. In the following lemma, we state the computational complexity for performing an exhaustive brute-force search for finding these r customers.

Lemma 1. *An exhaustive brute-force search for the set of r customers among n customers who are viewing a movie, such that these r customers are as evenly spaced (in movie times) as possible, requires $O(\frac{n!}{r(r-2)!(n-r)!})$ time.*

Proof: There are $C_r^n = \frac{n!}{r!(n-r)!}$ combinations of choosing r customers among n customers. For each of these combinations, it takes $r - 1$ subtractions to determine the distance among all pairs of consecutive customers. It thus takes $O(\frac{(r-1)n!}{r!(n-r)!})$ time steps to perform an exhaustive brute-force search. Note that in the worst case (when $r = \frac{n}{2}$), the exhaustive search has an exponential computational complexity[9] which can be shown by using Stirling's formula [8]. □

By Lemma 1, an exhaustive brute-force search for the best set of r piggybacking customers is computationally intensive. For example, if there are 25 customers viewing a movie at a node, and we want to choose 10 customers for piggybacking, we would need more than 29 million subtractions to determine the best set of choices. In view of the expensive computation required by an *exhaustive* search, we adopt the following heuristic algorithm

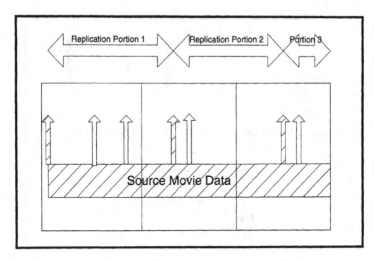

Figure 7. Choice of customers for piggybacking.

(see figure 7 for an illustration):

$r^* := \min(B_{n_t} - L_{n_t}(t), \phi)$
Divide the movie to be replicated into r^* equally
  spaced regions
For each region
  if the region is not empty of customers
    pick the earliest customer in that region

Note that r^* represents the maximum number of possible streams that can be generated for piggybacking replication, since a target node n_t for replication cannot support more than $B_{n_t} - L_{n_t}(t)$ additional streams, and we impose the hard limit ϕ on the number of replication streams. Since a straight forward implementation of the selection scheme would involve checking the progress of all customers viewing the movie at n_s, the algorithm possesses a complexity of $O(B_{n_s})$, which is a linear time algorithm.

To determine the replication time needed, consider a snapshot of the customers' progress in viewing the movie to be replicated at the time this algorithm is invoked, we can state the following result.

Lemma 2. *For a particular snapshot of the customer's process in viewing movie i, the replication time of a movie i under the piggybacked parallel replication policy, $\Upsilon_i(t)$, satisfies $\Upsilon_i(t) \leq (U_{i,x}(t) + 2)\frac{m_i}{r^*}$, where $U_{i,x}(t)$ denotes the largest number of consecutive regions present in the replica of movie i residing at node x that are empty of customers, m_i*

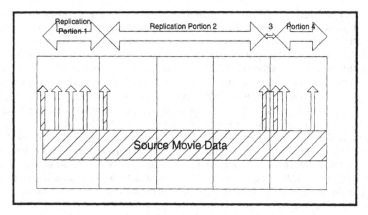

Figure 8. Illustration for Lemma 2.

denotes the length of movie i, r^* is the maximum number of possible streams that can be generated for piggybacked replication.

Proof: In the worst case, the piggybacked customer preceding the $U_{i,x}(t)$ empty regions would be at the beginning of the non-empty region to which it belongs, and the succeeding customer would be at the end of its region. The replication stream that is responsible for the largest part of the movie thus covers the $U_{i,x}(t)$ empty regions, plus two regions corresponding to the two customers bounding these regions. Each region takes $\frac{m_i}{r^*}$ time to replicate. Therefore the total replication time is bounded by $(U_{i,x}(t) + 2)\frac{m_i}{r^*}$. ☐

To illustrate, consider the figure 8 where four customers have been chosen for piggybacked replication of a movie divided into $r^* = 5$ regions, one of which is empty of customers (i.e., $U_{i,x}(t) = 1$). The second piggybacked customer is responsible for replicating the longest partition, which spans its own region, the empty region, and almost all of the succeeding region, because the third piggybacked customer is located near the end of its own region. In fact, the third piggybacked customer in this figure is responsible for a negligible fraction only. Note that, we expect the more significant discrepancies (in performance), between the heuristic and an optimal algorithm, to occur when the heuristic chooses fewer than r^* streams for piggybacking. However, in a very popular movie, which is the type of movie that should be replicated in any case, we expect the probability of such an occurance to be fairly low.

As in the case of piggybacked sequential replication policy causing problems with early acceptance, this policy causes problems with early migration. When the piggybacked customers issue VCR function requests, the early migrated customers may experience problems of movie data unavailability. The considerations in this case are essentially the same as in the case of early acceptance in piggybacked sequential replication.

3.3.5. Policy 5: Piggybacked & injected parallel replication.   Under the situations with an uneven distribution of customers at the source node, piggybacking is ineffective, causing the number of replication streams generated to be low, as explained in the previous section. Therefore, we propose the piggybacked & injected parallel replication policy, which aids in such cases by making use of the residual service capacities at the source and target nodes for injecting additional replication streams. Thus, under this policy, the number of replication streams is no longer tied to the customer distribution at the source node.

This execution of this policy is carried out in two stages. First, we follow the piggybacked policy to obtain a set of r customers for piggybacking. Then for the pair of consecutive piggybacked customers which are farthest apart, an extra replication stream is injected in the middle for reading of the movie data, thereby cutting the length of the longest partition for replication by half. This injection process is repeated to generate no more than $\tau = \min(B_{n_s} - L_{n_s}(t), B_{n_t} - L_{n_t}(t) - r, \phi - r)$ streams, which considers the residual service capacity at the source node n_s, the target node n_t, and the hard limit of replication streams. Figure 9 illustrates the effect of this policy with $r = 2$ and $\tau = 1$.

The overhead for the source and the target node would be τ and $\tau + r$ streams, respectively. Since the replication streams are responsible for different partitions of the movie, and because different partitions are of different lengths, they would complete at different times and therefore the overhead of replication at n_s and n_t would decrease gradually.

3.3.6. Policy 6: Multi-source injected & piggybacked parallel replication.   Although the policy in the previous subsection solves the problem of uneven distribution of customers available for piggybacking by compensating with additional injected streams, its success is largely dependent on the presence of residual service capacity at the source node. However,

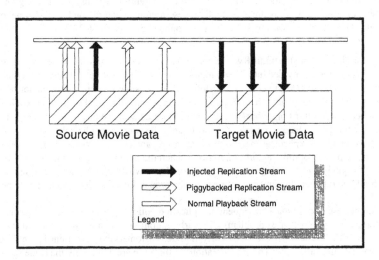

Figure 9.   Injected & piggybacked parallel replication.

46

since the need of replicating a movie implies that its available service capacity is low, it is likely that the source node possesses a limited amount of residual service capacity, and this is true especially if the movie being replicated is very popular. Since the lack of residual service capacities undermine the degree of parallelism and performance, we propose the multi-source injected & piggybacked parallel replication policy to extend replication model from using a single source node to using multiple source nodes. Under this policy, the combined residual service capacities at multiple source nodes can be exploited for higher degree of parallelism. Furthermore, the system will have more customers to choose from for piggybacking. This policy is also able to choose a more evenly distributed set of customers for piggybacking than the previous policies.

In order to carry out replication of movie i with this policy, some or all nodes in $R_i(t)$ are chosen to be source nodes. In this work, this choice is time-varying, i.e., the actual number of sources chosen is a function of the load on the nodes in $R_i(t)$, at the time of replication. The set of selected source nodes is static. Note that, with increasing number of nodes involved in replication, there would also be increasing overheads in the network resource (i.e, such as network buffer and network bandwidth) for the coordination of these nodes. Therefore, the limit on the number of source nodes should also depend on the available network resource; however, this is outside the scope of this paper. Once the source nodes are chosen, piggybacked replication streams are generated from the combined set of customers at the source nodes. Finally, injected replication streams are generated at the source nodes in a round-robin manner, such that the injection load is distributed evenly. The number of such streams to be generated depends on the residual service capacities available at the source nodes and the target node, as in the previous policy.

3.4. De-replication policy

It is crucial for our system to perform a *de-replication process* (i.e., removal of unnecessary movie replicas) before the system runs out of storage or bandwidth capacity, because at the time the system runs out of capacity, it will have to reject some of the arriving customer. Also, at the instant that the system runs out of resources, it may not be possible to initiate a movie replication process immediately by simply overwriting an existing replica of movie k. This is due to the fact that the system needs to migrate existing customers viewing movie k's replica to other nodes which contain another replica of movie k. In general, two issues must be addressed during the de-replication process: (1) which movie to de-replicate and (2) when to de-replicate that movie.

In our work, de-replication is invoked when the residual storage space in the whole system drops below a predefined threshold. When the popularity of a certain movie decreases, causing its number of replicas to be more than it currently needs, it becomes a suitable candidate for de-replication. Therefore, a replica of movie i at node x can be removed if and only if the following criteria are met:

- $A_i(t)/T_i(t) > 1$ where $T_i(t)$ is the replication threshold for movie i at time t. The rationale for this condition is that the number of replicas of movie i exceeds its current workload demand.

47

- The remaining replica nodes have sufficient residual service capacity to support the existing customers viewing the replica at node x, i.e., $\sum_{y \in (R_i(t) \setminus x)} (B_y - L_y(t)) > C_{i,x}(t)$, where $C_{i,x}(t)$ denotes the number of customers viewing movie i at node x.
- $A_i(t) - (B_x - L_x(t)) - C_{i,x}(t) > T_i(t) + D$, where D denotes the *de-replication threshold* parameter. With the removal of a replica at node x, $A_i(t)$ would be decreased by $(B_x - L_x(t) - C_{i,x}(t))$, since the existing customers viewing that replica would need to be served by other replicas. The resulting available service capacity must be greater than the replication threshold $T_i(t)$, otherwise the system might in the near future replicate a movie that has just been de-replicated. To prevent the system from oscillating between replication and de-replication, a de-replication threshold, $D > 0$, is introduced to impose a margin between the triggering threshold for replication and that for de-replication. (That is, we introduce hysteresis into the system.)

4. Experiments

Simulations are carried out to compare the performance of the different policies[10] proposed in Section 3. The performance metrics under study are the acceptance rate and the movie replication time. Beside evaluating the performance of the propose algorithms, we also try to answer the following questions. First, whether it is worthwhile to consume significant amount of resources (e.g., I/O bandwidth) for shortening the replication time with parallel replication technique and secondly, whether the movie popularity skewness affect the system's performance.

The system we consider consists of 20 nodes (i.e., $|S| = 20$), each node n_i has a storage capacity of 50 movies, and service capacity of 250 movie access streams. In our study, we use 500 distinct movies and each movie has a viewing duration of 90 minutes. Initially, there is one copy of each movie in the VOD system. The movies are assigned to nodes in a round-robin manner. For replication, a threshold limit h (refer to Section 3.1) of 0.7 is used. Viewing customer arrivals are modeled by a Poisson process with an average rate of $\lambda = a \times \frac{NB}{m}$ where N, B, m, and a are the number of nodes, node service capacity, the length of a movie, and the *relative* arrival rate with respect to the aggregate system service capacity, respectively. Let $p_{i+1} = \chi^i p_i$ for $0 \le i < 499$ be the popularity of movie $i + 1$ and χ is the degree of uniformly of move popularity. Unless otherwise stated, in the remainder of the paper we use $\chi = 0.618$ and $a = 1.0$ (i.e., maximum service capacity supported by the whole system). Note that in parallel replication strategies, the number of replication streams used during the replication process is time-varying. In general, the number of possible replication streams is determined by Eq. (6), where the hard limit is determined by the parameter ϕ.

4.1. Comparison of different policies

In this section, we compare the performance of various replication policies, and examine the effect of tuning various parameters of the replication algorithm. To isolate the performance of the various policies discussed in Section 3.3, in this section we disable the de-replication policy and keep the popularity distribution constant, which should result in a more fair comparison. To measure the performance of the different replication policies, we define the *acceptance rate* to be the number of accepted customers divided by the number of arrivals during the movie replication period. Mathematically, the movie replication period t^* is equal to:

$$t^* = \max_i \left\{ \min_t \{\tau_i \mid R_i(\tau_i) = R_i(t) \, \forall t \geq \tau_i \} \right\} \tag{7}$$

For ease of illustration, the lines in the legend of each figure are labeled in the same vertical order as they appear in the graph. The line labeled ''No Replication'' represents a system in which replication was suppressed, thus in this case there was only a single copy of each movie in the VOD system. The line labeled ''Upper Bound'' refers to an upper bound on our performance metric, namely, acceptance rate of 1.0, which is *unachievable* in practice.

Figure 10 illustrates the acceptance rate corresponding to the different replication policies. In general, the Injected & Piggybacked Parallel policy exhibits the best performance among the proposed policies. As expected, the sequential policies perform poorly because they exhibit significantly longer replication times and therefore, are not as responsive to the workload. The injected sequential policy and piggybacked sequential policy have similar performance because there is only a negligible overhead for the piggybacked sequential policy for this large scale VOD system. When the arrival rate is low, the difference on performance among the different policies are not too large due to the fact that the system is only lightly loaded.

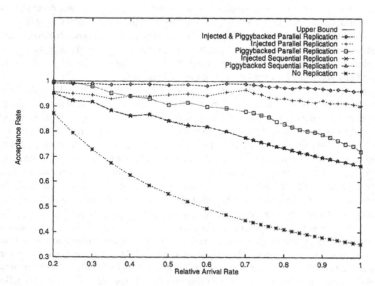

Figure 10.   Acceptance rate under various replication algorithms.

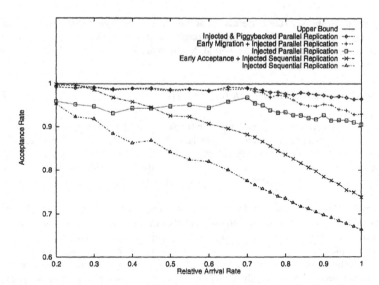

Figure 11.   Effect of early acceptance/migration.

Figure 11 shows the benefits of employing early acceptance or early migration, i.e., allowing customers to view incompletely replicated copies of some movies. As explained in Section 3.3.2 & Section 3.3.4, piggybacking-based replication policies are not good for early acceptance/migration due to complications with VCR functions. Therefore, early migration was applied to the injected parallel replication only, and early acceptance was applied to the injected sequential replication only. Here an improvement of $\approx 15\%$ can be achieved in some cases[11] through the use of these techniques.

Figure 12 depicts the replication time reduction achieved through parallel replication. The X-axis in this graph denotes the hard limit on the number of replication streams, ϕ. For example, the data points corresponding to the hard limit of 1 represent the case of sequential replication. It is clear that a higher number of (allowed) replication streams yields significantly shorter replication times. This translates to better acceptance rates as illustrated in figure 13, which gives an answer to the question on the tradeoff between using more resources for shortening replication time or using these resources for servicing viewing customers. Since the hard limit controls the maximum amount of resources that could be allocated to parallel replication, the fact that the acceptance rate grows with increasing limit implies that spending resources to shorten replication time is better. This is because addition of replicas has a long-term benefit over the short-term disadvantage of resource consumption. Under a high system load, however, there is a diminishing return in both figures because when the system is heavily loaded, there might be little residual capacity in the nodes that could be used for replication, thus limiting the number of replication streams. Therefore, these figures show appropriate value of ϕ so as to control the number of parallel replication streams. Note that figure 12 shows that with large values of ϕ, the injected & piggybacked replication policy outperforms the injected replication policy. On the other

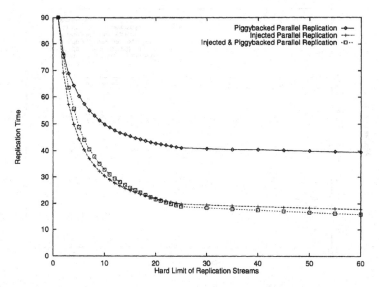

Figure 12.   Replication time.

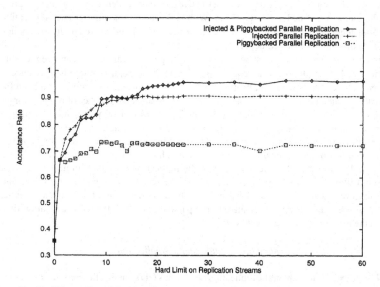

Figure 13.   Significance of parallel replication.

51

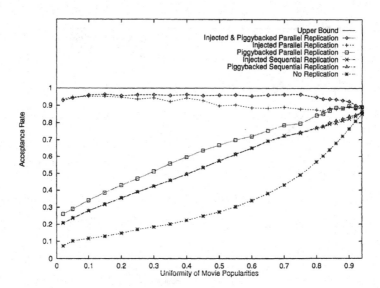

Figure 14.   Effect of varying movie popularities distribution.

hand, when the value of ϕ is low, the reverse is true. The reason is that with low values of ϕ, the injected & piggybacked replication policy allocates a large number of piggybacked replication streams, which are not always effective due to dependence on customer progress distribution, as explained in Section 3.3.4. With high values of ϕ, piggybacked replication could not generate as many replication streams as injected & piggybacked replication policy could, so the latter performed better.

Figure 14 illustrates how the skewness of movie popularities affects dynamic replication. When $\chi = 1$, all 500 movies are equally popular. In this case, the system performance is not sensitive to the choice of replication policy at all, because there simply is no need for replication, when the initial experiment setup provided an equal number of replicas for all movies.[12] The distinction between the replication policies is more pronounced when χ is low to moderate, i.e., the skewness in the movie popularity is high. In such situations, the policies that are able to replicate movies faster, for instance, the injected & piggybacked parallel replication, performed better and resulted in higher acceptance rates.

Figure 15 illustrates the effect of varying the replication threshold limit, h. When the threshold limit is too low, the responsiveness of the replication algorithm decreases and leads to lower acceptance rates. However, for policies which exhibit high replication time, the acceptance rate is fairly insensitive to the parameter h since the long replication time masks the algorithm's responsiveness to h.

4.2. Overall impact of dynamic replication and de-replication

To observe exactly how dynamic replication benefits a VOD system, other sets of simulations are carried out here with the notion of time varying movie popularities. The changing movie

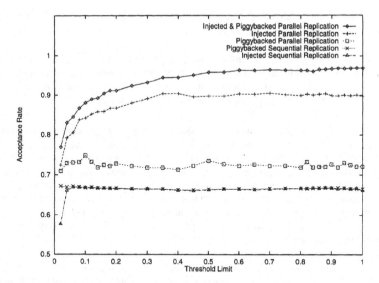

Figure 15.   Effect of varying threshold limit.

popularities necessitates the use of de-replication, otherwise the system storage would be exhausted by replicas of previously popular movies.

Specifically, we would like to investigate the effect of dynamic replication under the increase of movie popularities. Failure to cope with the change in movie popularity will result in the increase of rejection rate (or waiting time). Although increase of popularity in some movies is always coupled with decrease of popularity of other movies, the former change is more directly related to the acceptance rate. Therefore the following performance studies focus on the aspect of popularity increase instead of decrease. We consider two kinds of scenarios:

1. Gradual increase of popularities among movies—initially, some group of movies has the highest popularities. However, they become less popular gradually over time, while another group of movies becomes gradually more popular. This pattern corresponds to the change in types of audiences (and hence their interests) at different times throughout the day.
2. Drastic increase in popularities of movies—this scenario is mainly intended to test dynamic replication algorithms under the extreme cases. Although this could be thought of as addition of new and popular movies to the VOD system, in reality, a VOD service provider could usually anticipate the demand for new movies and prepare several copies before announcing their availability. Nevertheless, it is still interesting to see what would happen if there is unanticipated drastic increase of popularity of a movie, when only one copy of it is available originally. Such a scenario may happen in real life when a sequel

53

of an old movie comes out (e.g., people may want to watch the classic movie, *A Night to Remember*, after the popular movie *Titanic*.).

To simulate these scenarios, we "rotate" the movie popularities over time, with time $t = 0$ representing the initial instant. We define γ as the *rotation period* and shift the popularity of a movie to the next movie every γ units of time. With 500 movies arranged in a circular fashion, we have $p_i(t) = p_{(i-\lfloor \frac{t}{\gamma} \rfloor + 500) \bmod 500}(0)$ and we have two cases:

1. When $\gamma > 0$, movie popularities are increased gradually. To understand why, consider the initial condition ($t = 0$): $p_0(0) > p_1(0) > \cdots > p_{499}(0)$. At time $t = \gamma$, $p_0(t) = p_{499}(0)$, $p_1(t) = p_0(0)$, $p_2(t) = p_1(0)$, causing $p_1(t) > p_2(t) > \cdots > p_0(t)$. This means that movie 1, originally the second most popular movie, has its popularity increased slightly to become the most popular one. Movie 0, originally the most popular one, becomes unpopular. In general, with a positive γ, movies become more popular in a gradual fashion and some popular movies suddenly become unpopular.
2. When $\gamma < 0$, one movie will have its popularity drastically increased every time the popularities are rotated.

In our system, we set the de-replication threshold $D = 5$ and de-replication would be triggered when the system-wide aggregate residual storage capacity dropped below 30 movies. Simulation parameters are the same as before except that the storage capacity of a node is equal to 30 movies. Since 25 different movies would be stored in each node initially, this change reduced the initial free storage from 25 movies to 5 movies. The reason for this reduction of free space is to ensure that the effectiveness of the de-replication algorithm plays a significant role in system performance. If the VOD system can still offer good acceptance rates with this small amount of free storage under changing movie popularities, it would imply that the concept of dynamic replication is indeed practical and can be made effective using our proposed algorithms. Note that in the experiment, the statistics are averaged over a 7-day simulation period, to take into account the effects of both replication and de-replication, instead of the short movie placement reconfiguration period as measured in the previous set of experiments.

The simulation was carried out using the injected & piggybacked parallel replication policy with different values of γ. Figure 16 depicts the acceptance rates plotted against the absolute values of the rotation period, $|\gamma|$, in units of minutes. An increasing rotation period means that movie popularities were changed gradually. This allows higher acceptance rates because this situation allows more time for dynamic replication to adjust the movie configuration to match the demand well. The lines labeled "+ Direction" and "− Direction" show the acceptance rates achieved with dynamic popularities with positive values and negative values of γ, respectively. With positive values of γ, i.e., the movie popularities are increased gradually, the system generally offered high acceptance rates. As expected, the acceptance rates were generally lower with negative values of γ. This is because the system was under higher loading when unpopular movies would suddenly become very popular, creating a mismatch between the instantaneous movie configuration and the workload. Nevertheless, even at a rate as high as two movies with unanticipated drastic popularity

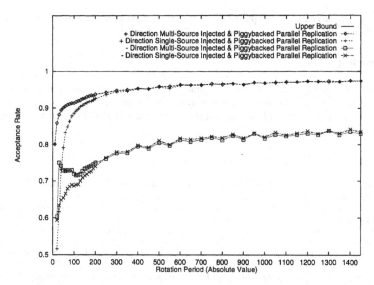

Figure 16. Dynamic movie popularities.

increase per day ($\gamma = -720$), the system still offers reasonable acceptance rates which are >80%.

As shown in the figure, the multi-source version of the replication policy offered higher acceptance rates when the change of popularities was very rapid, regardless of the direction of the popularity rotation. This is because with such rapid changes, dynamic replication could keep up with the demand only if the replication of movies could be finished in a short enough time, which would be a limiting factor for acceptance rates. Multi-source replication policies allow more replication streams to be utilized for replication, so replication time can be shortened considerably. As a result, they coped with rapid changes better. When the changes became less rapid, the replication time was no longer the limiting factor, thus they no longer showed significant improvement over their single-source counterparts.

5. Conclusions

In summary, we studied dynamic replication as an approach to address the problem of poor resource utilization and the complexity of handling heterogeneous disks in multi-node VOD systems. Several policies for triggering and performing replication were proposed and investigated. Our simulation results indicate that parallel replication policies perform best in terms of the increase in customer acceptance rate, since they shorten replication times and thereby improve the system performance. The high acceptance rates achieved by the policies studied in this paper indicates that dynamic replication is an effective approach in dealing with varying movie popularities. Therefore, without dynamic replication strategy, the VOD system may have a poor resource utilization problem.

Acknowledgments

The authors would like to thank the anonymous referees for their helpful and insightful comments. J.C.S. Lui was supported in part by the UGC Earmarked Grant and the CUHK Research Grant. L. Golubchik was supported in part by the NSF CAREER Grant CCR-96-25013.

Notes

1. The need to purchase additional disks can be due either to a growth in user demand or to disk failures and the need to replace those disks.
2. We use a simple model here in order to gain insight into the issues and tradeoffs associated with dynamic replication.
3. Note that, the data represented by each of the rectangular blocks in figure 1 is not necessarily logically-contiguous.
4. Instead of allowing customers to queue for service, immediate rejection is adopted for clearer indication of the performance results as shown in Section 4.
5. In what follows, we will mostly focus on the I/O bandwidth resources, since that is one of the important potential bottlenecks in a VOD system. In practice, other resources, such as the communication network bandwidth, should be considered; however, communication network issues are outside the scope of this paper.
6. The estimate of the replication time is based on the sequential replication algorithm which we will describe later.
7. The actual situation is much more complicated, due to customer departures, the existence of other movies in the same node and that the replication time can usually be reduced (to be described in Section 3.3). As a tradeoff for simpler computation, the proposed heuristic does not take these factors into account.
8. We assume that there is a non-negligible cost for transferring resources previously allocated to a movie replication process to a newly arrived viewing customer for a different movie.
9. Note also that this does **not** mean that the *problem* itself is NP-hard.
10. We would like to note here that many of the results presented in this section do not include a quantitative evaluation of policy 6. This is due to the fact that policy 6 is somewhat more complex than the other policies, and its (reasonably conclusive) study requires resolution of various issues that do not arise in the context of the other policies. For instance, such issues as "what is the optimal number of sources that should be used", "how should this number be adjusted dynamically, if at all", etc. These questions, as well as others, are part of on-going work and are outside the scope of this paper.
11. We should note that it is difficult, at this point, to make conclusive remarks on the utility of early acceptance/migration. This is partly due to the fact that the resulting performance gains are significantly affected by the "goodness" of the approach used in making decisions about when, during the replication process, to allow early acceptance. A study of this issue is part of our on-going work but is outside the scope of this paper.
12. No data points were plotted when χ became very close to 1.0, because no replication could take place, causing the period of movie placement reconfiguration to become undefined.

References

1. S. Berson, S. Ghandeharizadeh, R.R. Muntz, and X. Ju, "Staggered striping in multimedia information systems," in Proceedings of ACM SIGMOD '94, 1994, pp. 79–90.
2. T.L. Casavant and J.G. Kuhl, "A taxonomy of scheduling in general-purpose distributed computing," IEEE Transactions on Software Engineering, Vol. 14, No. 2, pp. 141–154, 1988.

3. M.S. Chen, H.I. Ssiao, C.S. Li, and P.S. Yu, "Using rotation mirrored declustering for replica placement in a disk-array-based video server," in Proceeding of the ACM Multimedia Conference, 1995, pp. 121–130.
4. A. Dan and D. Sitaram, "An online video placement policy based on bandwidth to space ratio (BSR)," in Proceedings of ACM SIGMOD'95, 1995.
5. A. Dan, M. Kienzle, and D. Sitaram, "A dynamic policy of segment replication for load-balancing in video-on-demand servers," ACM Multimedia Systems, Vol. 3, 1995.
6. L. Golubchik and J.C.S. Lui, "Bounding of performance measures for a threshold-based queueing system with hysteresis," in Proceedings of the ACM SIGMETRICS Conference, 1997, pp. 147–157.
7. R.R. Muntz and J.C.S. Lui, "Performance analysis of disk arrays under failure," in Proceedings of the 16th VLDB Conference, 1990, pp. 162–173.
8. R. Nelson, Probability, Stochastic Processes, and Queueing Theory, Springer-Verlag, 1995.
9. S.D. Stoller and J.D. DeTreville, "Storage replication and layout in video-on-demand servers," in Proceedings of NOSSDAV '95, 1995.
10. N. Venkatasubramanian and S. Ramanathan, "Load management in distributed video servers," in Proceedings of International Conference on Distributed Computing Systems, May 1997, pp. 528–535.
11. J.L. Wolf, P.S. Yu, and H. Shachnai, "DASD dancing: A disk load balancing optimization scheme for video-on-demand computer," in ACM SIGMETRICS Conference, 1995, pp. 157–166.

Peter W.K. Lie graduated from the Chinese University of Hong Kong with a B.S. and M.Phil. degrees in Computer Science. Peter W.K. Lie is currently working on commercial interactive TV and Video-on-Demand systems in the industry. His research interests are in scalable multimedia systems and distributed systems. His hobbies include watching movies and keeping track of advances in PC hardware and software architecture.

John Chi-Shing Lui was born in Hong Kong. He received his Ph.D. in Computer Science from UCLA. During the summer of 1990, he participated in a parallel database project in the IBM Thomas J. Watson Research Center. After his graduation, he joined a team at the IBM Almaden/San Jose Laboratory and participated in research and development of parallel I/O architecture and file system project. He later joined the Department of Computer Science and Engineering of the Chinese University of Hong Kong. For the past several summers, he has been a visiting professor/researcher in computer science departments at UCLA, Columbia University, and the University of Maryland at College Park. His current research interests are in distributed multimedia systems, OS design issues, communication networks, and performance evaluation theory. His personal interests include general reading and movies.

Leana Golubchik is currently an Assistant Professor in the Department of Computer Science at the University of Maryland at College Park; from Fall of 1995 until Summer of 1997, she was an Assistant Professor in the Department of Computer Science at Columbia University. Her current research interests are in the areas of multimedia information systems, high performance I/O, and computer systems modeling and performance evaluation. Leana received the B.S., the M.S., and the Ph.D. from the Computer Science Department at UCLA in 1989, 1992, and 1995, respectively. She is a guest co-editor for special issues of the Parallel Computing journal and the International Journal of Intelligent Systems, a program co-chair of MIS'99, as well as a program committee member of several conferences, including SIGMETRICS, SIGMOD, ICDCS, ICDE, EDBT, and PDIS. Leana has received several awards, including the NSF CAREER award, the IBM Doctoral Fellowship, and the NSF Doctoral Fellowship. She is a member of Tau Beta Pi, ACM, and IEEE.

Query Processing Techniques for Multimedia Presentations

T. LEE* tlee@ces.cwru.edu
L. SHENG sheng@ces.cwru.edu
N.H. BALKIR balkir@ces.cwru.edu
A. AL-HAMDANI ahamdani@ces.cwru.edu
G. ÖZSOYOĞLU tekin@ces.cwru.edu
Z.M. ÖZSOYOĞLU meral@ces.cwru.edu
Department of Computer Engineering and Science, Case Western Reserve University, Cleveland, OH 44106, USA

Abstract. A multimedia presentation is a synchronized, and possibly interactive, delivery of multimedia data to users. We expect that, in the future, multimedia presentations will be stored into and queried from multimedia databases. In an earlier work, we have designed a graphical query language, called GVISUAL, that allows users to query multimedia presentations based on content information. In this paper, we discuss GVISUAL query processing techniques for multimedia presentations. More specifically, we discuss the translation of GVISUAL queries into an operator-based language, called O-Algebra, with three new operators, and efficient implementations of the new O-Algebra operators using a coding system called nodecodes.

Keywords: multimedia databases, query languages, query processing, multimedia presentations

1. Introduction

A multimedia presentation is a synchronized, and possibly interactive, delivery of multi-media data to users [30]. Presently, multimedia presentations, created by multimedia authoring tools such as Authorware, IconAuthor, and Quest [15, 22, 26] are used in many applications, e.g., computer-aided training, computer-aided learning, and online books. We believe that, in the future, multimedia presentations, extracted from electronic books, will be much more commonly used in digital libraries. Therefore, there is a need to store, query and play multimedia presentations from multimedia databases.

One can represent multimedia presentations as temporally-aligned directed acyclic graphs, for visual specification of multimedia presentations. While there are other multimedia presentation models in the literature such as petrinet-based [21] or constraint-based models, we believe that most of these models can be mapped into a graph-based one. For extensive reviews of alternative multimedia presentation models, please see [6, 12, 25, 29].

We model multimedia presentations directly as graphs in a multimedia database. So, our (object-oriented) data model includes graph, node, and edge classes whose objects represent, respectively, multimedia presentations, multimedia data, and precedence edges between multimedia data. Figure 1 illustrates a simple presentation, represented as a graph,

---

Present address: Kyungsan University, College of Natural Sciences, Information and Science Department of Management Information Systems, Jomchon-Dong, San 75-Bonji, Kyongsan-City, Kyongsangbuk-Do, Korea.

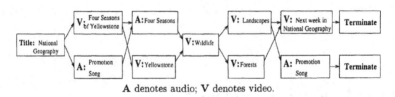

A denotes audio; V denotes video.

Figure 1.   Presentation "National Geography".

entitled "National Geography". We expect, from our experience with creating presentations [23, 27, 31], that multimedia presentation graphs are sparse, and do not have large number of nodes (e.g., 50 or less).

We envision, in the future, the existence of multimedia databases with "large" numbers of multimedia presentations, created and saved by users and usually derived from electronic books, electronic educational lecture materials, etc. Therefore, querying multimedia presentations based on content will also be important for the retrieval of desired presentations from a database of multimedia presentations. In [18], we have presented a data model, and discussed GVISUAL, which is an icon-based query language with a graphical interface, GOQL, a textual OQL-based language for graphs, and GCalculus/S which provides a formal basis for GVISUAL. Three temporal operators, *Next*, *Connected*, and *Until* from temporal logic are revised and used in GVISUAL, for the specifications of paths in multimedia presentations.

In this paper, we introduce techniques to process GVISUAL queries involving presentations. The contributions of this paper are listed below.

(1) Translating GVISUAL queries into an operator-based language: GVISUAL allows users to specify "paths" using icons corresponding to temporal operators *Next*, *Connected* and *Until*. In [19], we have described an object algebra language, called O-Algebra, for processing object-oriented queries. O-Algebra is an internal algebra, designed for an internal implementation (i.e., it is not for users to use directly). In this paper, we

   (a) give an internal, table-based representations of presentations. Each table is called a CO (Collection of Objects), and all presentations (graphs) are represented by a small number of CO's (tables).
   (b) extend O-Algebra with three temporal algebra operators MakeNext, MakeConnect and MakeUntil that use CO's and are algebraic, set-at-a-time versions of the GVISUAL operators *Next*, *Connected* and *Until*.
   (c) We give a direct translation from GVISUAL to O-Algebra.

(2) Implement the new O-Algebra operators efficiently: In [19], efficient O-Algebra implementations are discussed; therefore, here, we only consider the new graph operators of O-Algebra. Observing that presentations (graphs) are probably sparse and not very large (possibly, graphs with less than 50 nodes), we

    (a) propose the nodecode system which is based on Huffman Codes [14] and represents the path information for a presentation graph in compressed form,

    (b) give CO-based algorithms, with and without nodecodes, that implement the three new O-Algebra operators efficiently.

Run-time user interaction can be easily incorporated into a multimedia presentation using techniques from active and real-time databases [13, 17, 32]. More specifically, event-condition-action rules of active databases can be used to allow extensive user interaction during the playout of presentations in a time-constrained manner. For example, when a user presses a certain function key, a rule may triggered, and the associated action of the rule may allow the user to dynamically specify media synchronization such as freezing the playout of a video stream until another audio stream finishes its playout. In this paper, we do not deal with the user interaction issue for playout control.

GVISUAL and the techniques discussed in this paper are implemented on top of VISUAL on Windows NT, using Visual C++, Microsoft MFC Class Library and OLE-based drag-and-drop programming. Underneath VISUAL, we have developed a prototype client-server based database system, called ViSiOn, with a continuous multimedia server to deliver presentations [3].

In Section 2, we present the data model and its internal representation using CO's. Section 3 gives an overview of GVISUAL presentation (graph) operators. Section 4 presents the new operators of O-Algebra. Section 5 discusses the GVISUAL-to-O-Algebra transformation. In Sections 6 and 7, we discuss the nodecode system and the implementation of the new O-Algebra operators, with and without nodecodes. Section 8 summarizes ViSiOn, an OODBMS that contains GVISUAL as its query language. Section 9 briefly summarizes the related work, and Section 10 concludes.

2. Multimedia presentation data model and its internal representation using CO's

We now define the object-oriented data model we use. Each object o, defined below, has a *class (type)* c, and each class c has a number of *attribute names* associated with it. For simplicity, class represents both the class name and the structure of objects belonging to the class.

Multimedia presentations are directed acyclic graphs (DAG). From now on, we will use the terms presentation and presentation graph interchangeably. We now briefly describe presentation graphs[1] using an object-oriented data model. Each presentation stream is a node in the presentation graph, and edges describe sequential or concurrent playout of streams. Each presentation graph contains a *Title* (of type *Begin*) node and a node of type *Terminate*. The class Pres_Graph has attributes *Nodes* and *Edges*, which contain streams and their temporal ordering in a presentation graph. The attribute child_nodes of Pres_Node class contains oid's of streams temporally adjacent from each node object in Pres_Node. Each presentation graph edge may carry other information such as time delays. For simplicity in this paper, in a presentation graph, an edge carries no information except the notion of link between two nodes.

Multimedia data consists of media of type video, audio, text, still images and animation. In the following, we only give class definitions for the video data type as it is the richest multimedia data type. Each video stream consists of a sequence of representative Frames;[2] and each Frame has content objects (C-Objects) and content relationships among content objects. Please note that the same content object (with the same oid and the same value) *can* appear in multiple frames.

Content objects can be grouped into *primary content objects* and *background content objects*, or primary objects and background objects for short. For example, in a multimedia data, a video segment may have the objects *John-Doe, Red-Car* and *Indianapolis* with the relationship *John-Doe drives the Red-Car at Indianapolis.* John-Doe and Red-Car are primary objects. Indianapolis is a background object. An attribute of an object can have another object as its value, i.e., complex objects [9, 16] are allowed in our model.

In our model, we associate a valid time interval to an entire content object to represent the time of appearance of an object in video. Each appearance of a content object corresponds to an interval where the beginning and the end points of such an interval are the beginning and the end time points for the appearance of the content object in the video. For example, if object A appears at the time interval [09:10 Jan 1 1995, 09:30 Jan 1 1995], the temporal information is represented as [A, [09:10 Jan 1 1995, 09:30 Jan 1 1995]].

We modify and extend the relationships to represent a spatial relationship between two objects. We use the projected (on x and y axes) spatial relationships and the information about their overlap. We define all distinctive projected spatial relations between two objects along x and y coordinate axes.

In this paper, we use class extents Pres_Graphs, Pres_Nodes, Pres_Edges, Streams, Frames, C_Objects for the classes Pres_Graph, Pres_Node, Pres_Edge, Stream, Frame and C_Object, respectively. In order to internally represent the collection of instances of each object class, we use tables, called CO's (collection of objects), with (i) object id's (oids) and other attributes for each object, and (ii) at most one-level of nesting [19, 20]. Each CO has *only* one-level of nesting, and we map (possibly multilevel) objects of each class into one or more CO's. Object id's (oid's of objects) are retained in CO's.

```
class Pres_Graph type [            class Pres_Node : inherits
   name: String;                       from Stream
   other attributes;                   type [
   Nodes: {Pres_Node};                    graph-in: Pres_Graph;
   Edges: {Pres_Edge} ] ;                 child-nodes: {Pres_Node};
                                          parent-nodes: {Pres_Node};
class Stream type [                     other attributes ];
   name: String;
   type: String;                  class Frame type [
   pres_time: Real;                  name: String,
   rep_frame: <Frame>;               objects: {C_Object};
   no_of_frames: Integer;            other attributes ];
   topic: String;
   date: Date ];                  class C_Object type [
                                     name: String;
class Pres_Edge type                 frame-in: Frame;
   [<Pres_Node>];                     other attributes ];
```

Notation: "{ }" denotes the set constructor, and "< >" denotes the sequence constructor.

Figure 2. Object-oriented data model for presentation graphs.

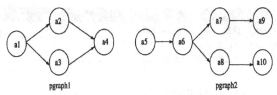

(a) Two presentation graphs

Pres_Edges

oid	
e11	<a1,a2>
e12	<a1,a3>
e13	<a2,a4>
e14	<a3,a4>
e21	<a5,a6>
e22	<a6,a7>
e23	<a6,a8>
e24	<a7,a9>
e25	<a8,a9>

Pres_Graphs

oid	name	nodes	edges
p11	pgraph1	{a1,a2 a3,a4}	{e11,e12 e13,e14}
p12	pgraph2	{a5,a6,a7, a8,a9,a10}	{e21,e22,e23 e24,e25}

Pres_Nodes

oid	name	graph-in	parent-nodes	child-nodes	rep-frames	....
a1	nature1	p11	*nil*	{a2,a3}	<fn1>	
a2	deer	p11	{a1}	{a4}	<f1,f2,f3>	
a3	buffallo	p11	{a1}	{a4}	<f17,f18>	
a4	end1	p11	{a2,a3}	*nil*	<fe1>	
a5	nature2	p12	*nil*	{a6}	<fn2>	
a6	Yosemite	p12	{a5}	{a7,a8}	<f21>	
a7	grizzly	p12	{a6}	{a9}	<f33,f34>	
a8	bird	p12	{a6}	{a10}	<f45>	
a9	end2	p12	{a7}	*nil*	<fe2>	
a10	end3	p12	{a8}	*nil*	<fe3>	

(b) CO's of objects belonging to Pres_Graphs,
Pres_Edges and Pres_Nodes classes

Figure 3.   Two presentation graphs and the corresponding CO's.

Example 2.1.   Assume that we have the two presentation graphs given in figure 3(a). Then, the corresponding CO's (collection of objects) are given in figure 3(b). Note that (i) the CO Pres_Nodes has three attributes graph_in, parent_nodes, and child_nodes that correspond to the adjacency list implementation of graphs, and (ii) the CO Pres_Graphs has two set-valued attributes, namely, nodes and edges, and thus has only one-level nesting. In figure 3, the two presentation graphs have oids p_{11} and p_{12}. We make the assumption that source nodes (i.e., nodes with no incoming edges; in figure 3, these are the nodes with oids a_1 and a_5) do not carry multimedia data. Similarly, sink nodes (i.e., nodes with no outgoing edges) a_4, a_9 and a_{10} also do not carry multimedia data.

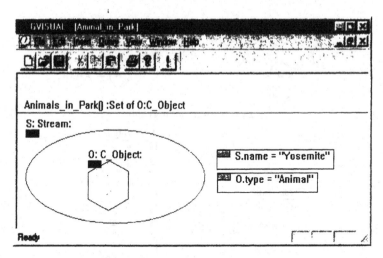

Figure 4. VISUAL query *Animals_in_Park*.

3. GVISUAL

This section summarizes only those features of GVISUAL [4, 5] relevant to the use and querying of presentation graphs. GVISUAL uses temporal operators *Next, Until* and *Connected* graphically in order to specify conditions involving presentation graph paths and nodes. A GVISUAL query is represented by one or more windows. Each query window is composed of a *query head* and a *query body*. Query head contains the name of the query (a unique name that distinguishes the query), *query parameters* (a list of input and output objects) and the output type specification. In figure 4, the main query is named *Animals_in_Park*, and has no input parameters. Each output parameter is defined with a name and a type specification (after the query name). Query output is always a CO. Query body consists of iconized objects, a condition box as well as internal/external queries (which are not discussed here).

Example 3.1.   In figure 4, the main query Animals_in_Park has one output parameter, namely, object O of type C_Object. The query output is a set of C_Object instances. The body of Animals_in_Park has the object S of type Stream, object O of type C_Object, and a condition box. The assertions specified in the condition box are (s_1.name = "Yosemite Park") and (O.type = "Animal").

Example 3.2.   In figure 5, the main query *YellowstonePresentation* has one output parameter, namely, object g_1 of type Pres_Graph. The query output is a set of Pres_Graph instances. The body of *YellowstonePresentation* has the object g_1 of Pres_Graph, the objects s_0, s_1, s_2 of type Stream, and a condition box with assertions.

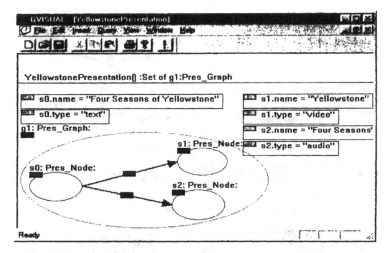

Figure 5. GVISUAL query *YellowstonePresentation.*

An object icon contains a variable name (or a constant), the corresponding type specification and an iconic representation. An object icon within another object represents a
composition relationship. We use the same two-dimensional window space to represent
both composition hierarchies and spatial relationships among data model objects [4, 5]. In
this paper, we do not deal with spatial relationships.

Users specify GVISUAL queries using the *interpretation semantics*. This means that,
for every instantiation of query variable objects with the corresponding data model objects
(or object components) in the database, methods and queries referred to within the query
body are evaluated, and conditions in the condition box are checked. The outputs are then
retrieved if all the conditions in the query are satisfied.

3.1. Icons and expressions

The semantics of temporal logic operators, namely, *Next, Until* and *Connected* in GVISUAL,
are different than their counterparts in temporal logic. Graphical constructs are used to
represent both temporal and non-temporal objects in a presentation graph in GVISUAL.
The icon shapes, colors and shading are chosen by the user and are arbitrary. For each non-
shaded icon, *var-name* (or *object-name*): *class-name* is associated. As an example, the oval
icon with label s_0: Pres_Node in figure 5 states that a variable object s_0 of type Pres_Node
exists.

For the specification of paths visually, we use different icons that represent an edge or a
path between two objects. A straight arrow with optional label P from object A to object
B (figure 6(a)) represents $Next(\mathcal{X})$, and states that, in the graph containing A and B, there
is an edge (also, a single-edge path) P from A to B. As an example, figure 6(d) states that
there is an edge from stream s_0 to stream s_1, and another edge from stream s_1 to stream s_2.

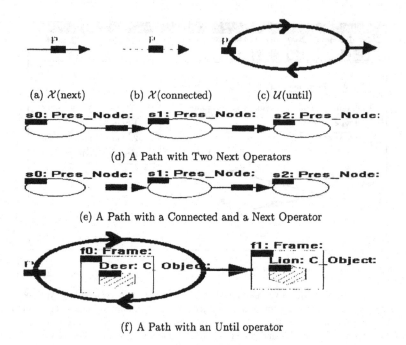

(a) $\mathcal{X}$(next)   (b) $\mathcal{X}$(connected)   (c) $\mathcal{U}$(until)

(d) A Path with Two Next Operators

(e) A Path with a Connected and a Next Operator

(f) A Path with an Until operator

Figure 6.   Three icons for the temporal relationships *Next*, *Connected* and *Until* and their use in path formulas.

A dashed arrow represents the *Connected* relationship (denoted by $\mathcal{C}$) and states that, in the graph containing A and B, there is a path P from A to B (figure 6(b)). As an example, figure 6(e) states that there is a path from stream s_0 to stream s_1, and an edge from stream s_1 to stream s_2.

A bold-faced oval with a solid arrow represents the *Until* relationship (denoted by $\mathcal{U}$) (figure 6(c)) and expresses repetition: starting at a node in a given presentation graph, a sequence of nodes repetitively satisfying a given assertion is encountered until a node satisfying another assertion is encountered. As an example, GVISUAL expression in figure 6(f) states that, starting at frame f_0 in a given stream (where f_0 is determined possibly through other conditions), f_0 and each consecutive frame contain the content object "Deer" until a frame f_1 with the content object "Lion" is encountered, and the resulting sequence (path) of frames constitutes P.

There are four semantic and syntactic differences between GVISUAL temporal operators and those of temporal logic [11].

(1) In temporal logic, formulas always apply starting from state 0 (at time 0) ("state" corresponds to "node" in a graph). In contrast, GVISUAL temporal operators (including

Next) can apply starting from any chosen node (i.e., state) in the graph for simpler specifications of formulas about paths in a presentation graph.

(2) GVISUAL uses the notion of *node variables* instantiated by nodes (e.g., streams s_0 and s_1 in figure 6(d)) which does not exist in temporal logic. The state (node) that is reached by temporal operators of temporal logic is identified *not* by the use of node variables, but, by the fact that temporal logic formulas always apply starting from a fixed state, i.e., state 0, and the state for which state formulas apply is clear from the use of temporal logic operators. The use of node variables allows GVISUAL to specify assertions in a straightforward manner.

(3) In temporal logic, the sequence of states (i.e., paths in graphs) satisfying a "path formula" can not be extracted and output. GVISUAL uses path variables to name and output such paths (e.g., the variable P in figure 6(a)–(c).

(4) The *Next* operator exploits the explicit specification of nodes and node variables, and, has *two* operands, e.g., for the *Next* icon from s_0 to s_1 in figure 7(a), (state) formulas

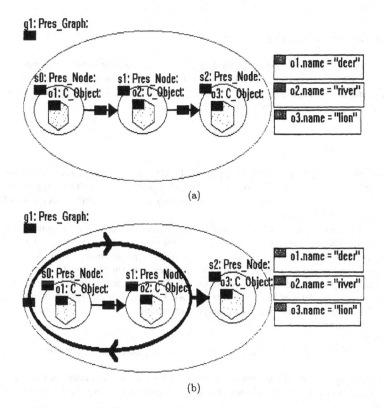

(a)

(b)

Figure 7. Containment relationship and path specification.

about the states s_0 and s_1 can be specified. In comparison, the *Next* operator of temporal logic [11] uses a single operand.

GVISUAL examples of figure 7 illustrate the use of containment relationships and path specifications simultaneously. Figure 7(a) denotes that the presentation graph g has three consecutive streams s_0, s_1 and s_2, which, respectively, satisfy the assertions "s_0 has a frame with the C_Object deer", "s_1 has a frame with the C_Object river", and "s_2 has a frame with the C_Object lion". The GVISUAL expression in figure 7(b) specifies that the presentation graph g_1 has a sequence of streams that start at s_0 and s_1, and repetitively satisfy the assertions "a stream has a frame with the C_Object deer" and "the next stream has a frame with the C_Object river", until the stream s_2 that satisfies the assertion "s_2 has a frame with the C_Object lion" is reached. Please note that whatever is specified inside the bold-faced oval of the *until* icon represents a *path formula* that is repetitively satisfied along a path (or a sequence).

4. An algebra for querying presentation graphs

O-Algebra [19, 20] is an object algebra designed for processing object-oriented database queries. O-Algebra operands are CO's. We extend O-Algebra with new operators that correspond to the graph operators $\mathcal{X}$, $\mathcal{C}$ and $\mathcal{U}$ so that we can translate and implement GVISUAL queries in an algebraic way.

4.1.   O-Algebra

This section summarizes only a subset of the O-Algebra [19, 20] operators needed to illustrate our extensions. Each operation in O-Algebra produces a new CO. O-Algebra has the traditional operators; select(σ), join($\bowtie$), project(π), union($\cup$) and difference(-) as well as other operators [19, 20].

O-Algebra uses the terminology *hpath* for a "heterogeneous path", i.e., a sequence of objects of possibly different types. More, specifically, the representation $S[x_1].A_1 \ldots A_k[x_{k+1}]$ or $S[x_1].A_1 \ldots A_k[x_{k+1}^*]$ is called an *hpath* over different types of objects, where S is a CO of type T, and x_1 and x_{k+1} are optional attribute names in S. The notation $T.A_1.A_2 \ldots A_k$ denotes the type obtained by tracing down the $A_1, A_2, \ldots, A_k$ properties from T. The notation $S.A_1 \ldots A_k$ denotes an extent of type $T.A_1.A_2 \ldots A_k$. For example in figure 8(d), the CO corresponds to the path Streams[s].rep-frames.objects[o], and is obtained by the O-Algebra expression

$$\text{Remap}_{(rep-frames,s,rep-frames)}(Streams) \bowtie \text{Remap}_{(objects,rep-frames,o)}(Frames)$$

where $\text{Remap}_{(a,b,c)}(R)$ (illustrated in figure 8(c)) flattens the set-valued attribute a of the CO R, names the newly-flattened attribute as b, and retains the oid attribute of R as attribute c.

	Streams	
oid	name	rep-frames
s1	n1	<f1,f2>
s2	n2	<f3>

Frames

oid	objects
f1	{o1,o2}
f2	{o3}
f3	{o4}

(a)   (b)

Streams[s].rep-frames.objects[o]

$\text{Remap}_{(rep-frames,b,c)}(Streams)$

oid	b	c
r1	s1	f1
r2	s1	f2
r3	s2	f3

oid	s	rep-frames	o
h1	s1	f1	o1
h2	s1	f1	o2
h3	s1	f2	o3
h4	s2	f3	o4

(c)   (d)

Note: For simplicity, CO's of above figures
do not show all the attributes.

Figure 8. CO's corresponding to *Streams, Frames,* Remap$_{(rep-frames,b,c)}$(*Streams*) and hpath Streams[s].rep-frames.objects[o].

4.2. New algebra operators: X^{Next}, $X^{Connected}$ and X^{Until}

To translate the temporal operators in GVISUAL queries, we need new O-Algebra operators that build paths (over presentation graphs) satisfying the relationships specified by the temporal operators. We now define set-at-a-time operators, called *path algebra operators*, which directly correspond to temporal operators in GVISUAL queries.

We first define the terminology.

Definition 4.1.

(a) When there is an edge from the last node of path p_1 to the first node of path p_2, we say that path p_1 is *adjacent to* path p_2.

(b) When there is a directed path from the last node of path p_1 to the first node of path p_2, we say that path p_1 is *connected to* path p_2.

(c) When path p_1 is connected to path p_2 through path cp, which is a path with zero or more nodes, we say that path cp is *the connecting path*.

(d) Consider paths $p_1, \ldots, p_n$. The notation $p_1 \cdot \ldots \cdot p_n$ denotes the *construction* of a new path by concatenating $p_1, \ldots, p_n$ in the order of $p_1, \ldots, p_n$. That is, the last node of p_i is *made* adjacent to the first node of p_{i+1}, $1 \le i \le n - 1$, by adding an edge from the last node of p_i to the first node of p_{i+1}.

We now define the new algebra operators. Let A and B be CO's with attributes g_1 and g_2, respectively, containing graph oid's (object identifiers). Let p_1 and p_2 be attributes of type list in COs A and B, respectively, and containing paths in graphs specified in attributes g_1 and g_2, respectively. For a path instance p, *First*(p) and *Last*(p) denote the first and

69

the last node instances, respectively, in p. If node n_1 is adjacent (connected) to node n_2 in graph g then the predicate $Nxt(n_1, n_2, g)$ $(Cnected(n_1, n_2, p, g)$ where p is a path in g) is true. Both predicates $Nxt()$ and $Cnected()$ can be evaluated using the information in the CO $Pres\_Nodes$. Finally, for a given node n in a graph g, the method $Children(n)$ returns the set of nodes in g that are adjacent from n.

- $MakeNext(X^{Next})$: The $MakeNext$ operator $A \ X^{Next}_{(g_1,g_2,p_1,p_2,p)} \ B$ outputs a CO which has (i) a new attribute p and (ii) all the attributes of A and B except p_1, p_2 and g_2.

$$A \ X^{Next}_{(g_1,g_2,p_1,p_2,p)} \ B = \{ \ [g: a.g_1, \ p: a.p_1 + b.p_2 \ AllOtherAttributesInAandB]$$
$$|a \in A, b \in B, a.g_1 = b.g_2, Nxt(Last(a.p_1), First(b.p_2), g_1) \ \}$$

That is, let a and b be two tuples in A and B, respectively. If a and b refer to the same graph (i.e., $a.g_1 = b.g_2$) and the last node of $a.p_1$ is adjacent to the first node of $b.p_2$ then X^{Next} outputs a tuple with a new attribute that contains the path $a.p_1 + b.p_2$.

- $MakeConnect(X^{Connected})$: The $MakeConnect$ operator $A \ X^{Connected}_{(g_1,g_2,p_1,p_2,p)} \ B$ outputs a CO which has (i) a new attribute p and (ii) all the attributes of A and B except p_1, p_2 and g_2.

$$A \ X^{Connected}_{(g_1,g_2,p_1,p_2,p)} \ B = \{ \ [g: a.g_1, \ p: a.p_1 * p_c * b.p_2 \ AllOtherAttributesInAandB]$$
$$|a \in A, b \in B, a.g_1 = b.g_2, p_c \in C,$$
$$C = \{p'|Cnected(Last(a.p_1), First(b.p_2), p', g_1)\} \ \}$$

That is, let a and b be two tuples in A and B, respectively. If a and b refer to the same graph (i.e., $a.g_1 = b.g_2$) and the last node of $a.p_1$ is connected to the first node of $b.p_2$ (by, say, path p_c) then $X^{Connected}$ outputs a tuple with a new attribute that contains the path $a.p_1 * p_c * b.p_2$.

- $MakeUntil$ (X^{Until}): The $MakeUntil$ operator $A \ X^{Until}_{(g_1,g_2,p_1,p_2,p)} \ B$ outputs a CO which has (i) a new attribute p and (ii) all the attributes of A and B except p_1, p_2 and g_2.

$$A \ X^{Until}_{g_1,g_2,p_1,p_2,p} B = \{ \ [\ g: a.g_1, \ p: (a_1.p_1).(a_2.p_1). \ldots . (a_k.p_1).(b.p_2),$$
$$AllOtherAttributesInAandB \ ]$$
$$|\exists a_1, a_2, \ldots, a_k \in A, b \in B, \forall 1 \leq i \leq k, a_i.g_1 = b.g_2, \forall 1 \leq i < k,$$
$$First(a_{i+1}) \in Children(Last(a_i)), First(b) \in Children(Last(a_k)) \ \}$$

Example 4.1. Consider figure 9, where we have the CO's P (figure 9(b)) and Q (figure 9(c)) obtained perhaps through other O-Algebra operators, and we give the output CO's for X^{Next} (figure 9(d)), $X^{Connected}$ (figure 9(e)) and X^{Until} (figure 9(f)) using the presentation graph of figure 9(a).

5. GVISUAL to O-Algebra translation

For an efficient implementation, GVISUAL is directly translated into O-Algebra. Balkir et al. [2] provides a method to translate VISUAL into an algebra expression, which uses

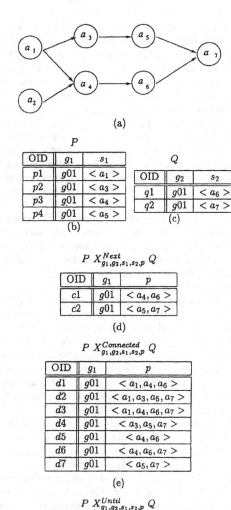

(a)

P

OID	g_1	s_1
$p1$	$g01$	$< a_1 >$
$p2$	$g01$	$< a_3 >$
$p3$	$g01$	$< a_4 >$
$p4$	$g01$	$< a_5 >$

(b)

Q

OID	g_2	s_2
$q1$	$g01$	$< a_6 >$
$q2$	$g01$	$< a_7 >$

(c)

$P\ X^{Next}_{g_1,g_2,s_1,s_2,p}\ Q$

OID	g_1	p
$c1$	$g01$	$< a_4, a_6 >$
$c2$	$g01$	$< a_5, a_7 >$

(d)

$P\ X^{Connected}_{g_1,g_2,s_1,s_2,p}\ Q$

OID	g_1	p
$d1$	$g01$	$< a_1, a_4, a_6 >$
$d2$	$g01$	$< a_1, a_3, a_5, a_7 >$
$d3$	$g01$	$< a_1, a_4, a_6, a_7 >$
$d4$	$g01$	$< a_3, a_5, a_7 >$
$d5$	$g01$	$< a_4, a_6 >$
$d6$	$g01$	$< a_4, a_6, a_7 >$
$d7$	$g01$	$< a_5, a_7 >$

(e)

$P\ X^{Until}_{g_1,g_2,s_1,s_2,p}\ Q$

OID	g_1	p
$h1$	$g01$	$< a_1, a_4, a_6 >$
$h2$	$g01$	$< a_1, a_3, a_5, a_7 >$
$h3$	$g01$	$< a_3, a_5, a_7 >$
$h4$	$g01$	$< a_4, a_6 >$
$h5$	$g01$	$< a_5, a_7 >$

(f)

Figure 9. CO's after applying operators X^{Next}, $X^{Connected}$ and X^{Until}.

the complex algebra operators of Deshpande and Larson [10]. We adopt and revise this translation, i.e., instead of the complex algebra, we use the O-Algebra and provide a way to translate icons corresponding to the temporal operators $\mathcal{X}$, $\mathcal{C}$ and $\mathcal{U}$ to an O-Algebra expression as well as a way to translate the visual specification and formulas in a condition box of GVISUAL. Next we briefly summarize the GVISUAL parse tree construction process [1, 2].

GVISUAL parse trees are constructed bottom-up. The algorithm to construct the parse tree uses the following steps. The first step is the construction of the main parse tree using the objects that are specified in the main query, the composition relationships between the objects, and the temporal logic operators between these objects. A graph is created from the composition hierarchy by inserting edges from contained objects to container objects. Each path that starts either at a root node or at a leaf node in the resulting graph defines a CO_hpath. Then, the edges that correspond to temporal operators are added to the graph. These edges are from the starting object of the temporal operator to the ending object of the temporal operator.

Next, a topological sort is applied to the graph. The result of the topological sort creates the main parse tree. The third step is to construct a parse tree for each input parameter (if any). A node is created for every input parameter, and appended to the main parse tree of the query. The fourth step is to construct a parse tree for each internal and external subquery in the main query, and add it to the parse tree of the main query.

Parse tree construction for a subquery is similar to parse tree creation for the main query. To add the parse tree for the subquery to the parse tree for the main query, results of the subquery pass through a grouping on the input parameters and an outer join with the main query parse tree. The fifth step is to add the conditions in condition boxes to the parse tree of the main query. If the condition box does not contain a subquery expression, a selection node is created in the parse tree. This selection is then pushed down the parse tree for efficiency. If a cartesian product node is found during the push-down of the selection node, both nodes are replaced by a join node for efficiency. The sixth step is to add methods to the parse tree of the main query. Finally, in the seventh step, the output parameters are projected from the parse tree, and the return type of the query is specified.

The rest of this section discusses only the translation of path formulas in GVISUAL into path algebra operators of O-Algebra. We illustrate how to translate containment and temporal relationships specified in the query body as visual specifications, and how to put them together as a whole to obtain the final O-Algebra expression.

Consider a visual specification in a GVISUAL query where two relationships, containment relationship and temporal relationship, are expressed. First, we obtain a CO that corresponds to an hpath and whose tuples satisfy the containment relationship. Second, we apply O-Algebra operators corresponding to temporal relationships with the CO as an operand. Each path algebra operator adds attributes, whose values are paths satisfying the temporal relationships, to the input CO.

5.1. Containment relationships

An object inside another object in a GVISUAL query specifies a containment relationship. In terms of the object-oriented data model, it represents the composition hierarchy. The dereferencing of the composition hierarchy in O-Algebra is expressed by a CO_hpath expression. The way to obtain the CO corresponding to a CO_hpath is as follows: Each object icon in the GVISUAL query body becomes a node in a containment tree. The outermost object becomes a root. The nodes for icons that are immediately contained in the root icon are attached as children. This process continues iteratively for every object icon. When the icons that are immediately contained in an icon are not consistent with the data model, we add the relationship that is missing in the query body to the trees. For example, in figure 10(a), the stream s contains the content objects o_1 and o_2 while a stream contains frames, and a frame contains content objects in the data model. Figure 10(a) and (b) have the same containment tree representation as in figure 10(c).

In the containment tree representation, each path from a root node to a leaf node represents a CO_hpath. In figure 10(c), there are two paths, from the node (g: Pres_Graph) to the leaf nodes (o_1: C_Object, o_2: C_Object). The algebra expressions of the paths are the ones corresponding to the CO_hpath(Pres_Graphs[g].Nodes[s].rep_frame[f].objects[o_1]) and CO_hpath(Pres_Graphs[g].Nodes[s].rep_frame[f].objects[o_2]).

5.2. Temporal relationship

After translating the containment relationships, the tuples of the resulting CO satisfy the containment relationship. Then, we apply O-Algebra operators corresponding to temporal relationships. The operand of the first operator is a CO satisfying the containment relationships.

Among the temporal operators, there may exist a precedence order. When an icon for a temporal relationship is inside another icon for a temporal relationship, there is a precedence order to be observed among the operators corresponding to the temporal relationships. When there is a precedence order, we apply the operator corresponding to a temporal relationship specified innermost and continue to apply operators corresponding to other temporal relationships specified immediately next to the relationship moving outward.

Example 5.1. In the GVISUAL query given in figure 12, there is a *Next* relationship inside an *Until* relationship and, we must apply X^{Next} before applying X^{Until}.

5.3. Examples

We now give two example GVISUAL queries and their evaluation parse trees.

Example 5.2. The query in figure 5 outputs presentation graphs having a text stream with name "Four Seasons of YellowStone", followed concurrently by a video stream and an audio stream with names "YellowStone" and "Four Seasons", respectively.

We illustrate the evaluation of the query using the evaluation parse tree of figure 11 (The full parse tree created by an actual GVISUAL run is given in Appendix A, figure A1.). Let the three CO's, say $CO_0(g_1, s_0)$, $CO_1(g_1, s_1)$ and $CO_2(g_1, s_2)$, correspond to the CO_hpaths, representing the containment relationships Pres_Graphs[g_1].Nodes[s_0],

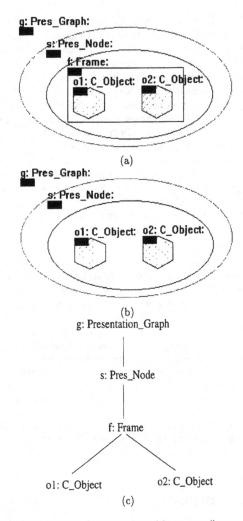

Figure 10. Containment relationship: iconic representation and the corresponding parse tree.

Pres_Graphs[g_1].Nodes[s_1] and Pres_Graphs[g_1].Nodes[s_2], respectively. The values of the attributes g_i and s_i are oid's of objects belonging to classes Pres_Graph and Pres_Node. From the selection operations, we select streams satisfying the formulas in the condition box. The next set of join operations produce CO's whose tuples satisfy the formulas in the condition box and the containment relationships. Finally, the two X^{Next} operations produce

74

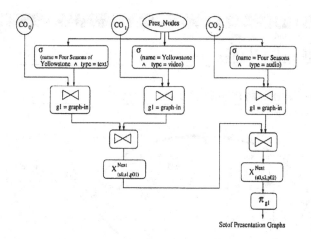

Figure 11. Evaluation parse tree of the GVISUAL query YellowstonePresentation (in figure 5).

a CO whose tuples contain a graph and three streams, satisfying the temporal relationships, in the graph. The projection operation outputs presentation graphs.

Example 5.3. The query in figure 12 outputs presentation graphs with a sequence of adjacent stream pairs (s_1, s_2) until a stream with the name "Presidential Election" is encountered. The stream s_1 contains a frame with the object "Bill Clinton", and the stream s_2 contains a frame with the object "Bob Dole".

We illustrate the evaluation of the query using the evaluation parse tree of figure 13 (The full parse tree created by an actual GVISUAL run is given in Appendix A, figure A2.). Let the three CO's, say $CO_1(g_1, s_1, f_1, o_1)$, $CO_2(g_1, s_2, f_2, o_2)$ and $CO_3(g_1, s_3)$, correspond to the CO_hpaths representing the containment relationships Pres_Graphs[g_1].Nodes[s_1]. rep_frame[f_1].objects[o_1], Pres_Graphs[g_1].Nodes[s_2].rep_frame[f_2].objects[o_2] and Pres_Graphs[g_1].Nodes[s_3], respectively. The values of the attributes g_i, s_i, $i = 1, 2$, f_j, $j = 1, 2, 3$ and o_k, $k = 1, 2$, are oid's of objects belonging to the classes Pres_Graph, Pres_Node, Frame and C_Object classes. Each tuple in one of the above CO's contains a graph, a stream in the graph, a frame in the stream and a content object in the frame, respectively, i.e., the values in each tuple satisfy the containment relationships. Using selection operations, we select content objects satisfying the formulas in the condition box. The following join operations produce CO's which satisfy the formulas in the condition box and the containment relationships. Finally, X^{Next} and X^{Until} operations produce a CO whose tuples contain a graph, three streams in the graph, two frames in the two streams and two C_Object objects in the frames (where C_Objects satisfy the temporal relationships). The projection operation outputs presentation graphs.

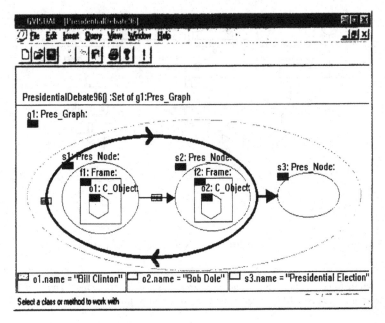

Figure 12. GVISUAL query PresidentialDebates96.

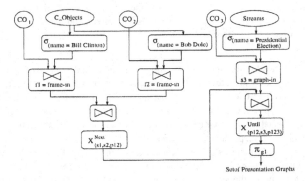

Figure 13. Evaluation parse tree of the GVISUAL query PresidentialDebates96 (in figure 12).

6. Node code system for representing presentation graphs

In a presentation query, the operations to evaluate the query include traversals of presentation graphs. Algorithms that confirm the adjacency and the connectiveness between nodes efficiently are required to implement operators X^{Next}, $X^{Connected}$ and X^{Until}.

One way to traverse presentation graphs is to use the CO's and employ a modified conventional depth-first search algorithm, i.e., given two paths, say p_1 and p_2, by using the tuples of CO's directly, we visit every node along the paths starting from the last node of p_1 and check if we encounter the first node of p_2. This way, one can implement the operator $X^{Connected}$. However, this may lead to inefficient implementations. Next, we propose a much faster approach.

Based on the observation that presentation graphs are not expected to be too large (e.g., less than 50 nodes and sparse graphs), we now propose a new scheme, called the *nodecode* system, to represent presentation graphs. In the nodecode system, we assign unique codes to every node. A node which appears on multiple paths is assigned multiple distinct codes. Given the nodecodes of a node a, nodecodes of all nodes reachable from a can be derived by bit manipulations on the nodecodes, *without any graph traversal*. The nodecodes of two nodes can tell whether there is a path between two nodes, and, if a path exists then it can be derived without any graph traversals.

6.1. The structure of the node code system

We now illustrate how we assign unique nodecodes to nodes of a presentation graph. We first transform a presentation graph, which is a directed acyclic graph with a single source node,[3] into the corresponding directed acyclic binary graph (DABG) whose nodes have at most two outgoing edges with edges distinguished as *down* (child) or *right* (sibling) edges. Figure 14 illustrates a presentation graph and the corresponding DABG. In a DABG, the down edge is used to represent a parent-child relationship and the right edge is used to represent a sibling relationship.

A presentation graph is transformed into the corresponding DABG using the following rules: (1) For each node in the presentation graph, there is a corresponding node in the DABG. (2) When there are multiple child nodes of a node in a presentation graph, in the corresponding DABG, one child is connected to the parent by a down edge, and the rest of the siblings are made adjacent to each other by right edges.

Assume that the longest path in a DABG is of length $(n - 1)$. Then we reserve n bits to represent each node of the DAGB. Insert 1 at the leftmost bit, and insert 0 for each

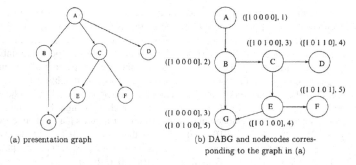

(a) presentation graph

(b) DABG and nodecodes corresponding to the graph in (a)

Figure 14.   A presentation graph and its DABG.

down edge and 1 for each right edge along a path starting from the source node to a node. For a given node, the binary code obtained by concatenating 0's and 1's along the path to the node and padded on the right by 0's for the rest of the n bits, is called the *node number* of the node. If a non-source node appears in multiple paths, the node is assigned multiple different node numbers. Clearly, the source node has the node number $10\ldots0$ with $(n-1)$ 0's.

For an n-digit node number, we call the leftmost k digits, $k \leq n$, due to the traversal from the source node to the corresponding node, *k-effective digits* of the node. For a given node in the DABG, its nodecode is the two-tuple (node number, k = the corresponding effective digits), which are illustrated in figure 14(b). As an example, the node C in figure 14(b) has 3-effective digits 1, 0 and 1, i.e., the leftmost three digits of the node number. Note that some nodes have the same node number, which means that the node number alone can not determine the position of a node in a path or in the presentation graph. So, we complement the node number with the effective digit information. If there are multiple node numbers for a node, then there are the corresponding multiple effective digits.

The following are some useful properties of nodecodes.

Remark 1. Let (c, k) denote the node number and the k-effective digits of a given node. Then the nodecode (c, k) in a binary acyclic directed graph is unique.

Definition 6.1. Given two nodecodes, $N_1 = (c_1, k_1)$ and $N_2 = (c_2, k_2)$, $N_1 = N_2$ when $(c_1 = c_2) \wedge (k_1 = k_2)$, and $N_1 > N_2$ when $(c_1 > c_2)$ or $(c_1 = c_2) \wedge (k_1 > k_2)$.

Remark 2. Consider the node v with the nodecode $(a_1 a_2 \ldots a_l 0 \ldots 0, l)$. Then, the node-codes of v's children are $(a_1 a_2 \ldots a_l 0 \ldots 0, (l+1))$ $(a_1 a_2 \ldots a_l 0_{l+1} 1_{l+2} 0 \ldots 0, (l+2))$, ..., $(a_1 a_2 \ldots a_l 0_{l+1} 1_{l+2} \ldots 1_m 0 \ldots 0, m)$ where the node v has $(m-l)$ child nodes.

Remark 3. Consider the node v with the nodecode $(a_1 a_2 \ldots a_l 0 0 \ldots 0, l)$. Then, the node-codes of nodes which are connected from v are greater than or equal to the nodecode $(a_1 a_2 \ldots a_l 0 0 \ldots 0, (l+1))$, called the *lo_code* of the node v, and less than the nodecode $(a_1 a_2 \ldots a_l 1_{l+1} 0 \ldots 0, (l+1))$, called the *hi_code* of the node v.

Proof: Assume that there are k nodes which are immediate children of v. The node code of the child node adjacent from v through the down edge is $(a_1 a_2 \ldots a_l 0 0 \ldots 0, (l+1))$, which is the smallest node code among node codes of v's descendants because all other descendants have larger node numbers and larger effective digits. Consider the node numbers of the k immediate children of v, i.e., one node is adjacent from the parent node through the down edge and each node of the other $(k-1)$ nodes is adjacent to its sibling through its sibling edge. Then the node number of the k_{th} immediate child node, which has no adjacent right siblings, is $(a_1 \ldots a_l 0 1 \ldots 1 0..0)$ with $(k-1)$ 1's, which is the highest node number among all descendants of v. The node number of a sibling of v through a right edge from v is $(a_1 a_2 \ldots a_l 1 0 \ldots 0)$. $(a_1 a_2 \ldots a_l 1 0 \ldots 0)$ is greater than $(a_1 \ldots a_l 0 1 \ldots 1 0..0)$ (with $(k-1)$ 1's). Thus the node codes of nodes connected from v are greater than or equal to $(a_1 a_2 \ldots a_l 0 0 \ldots 0, (l+1))$ and less than $(a_1 a_2 \ldots a_l 1 0 \ldots 0, (l+1))$.   □

Remark 4. Assume that we reserve n bits for nodecodes. If the nodecode of a node v is (m, k), where m is a decimal number and k is v's effective digits, then nodecodes of v's child nodes are $(m, (k + 1))$, $((m + 2^{n-k-2}), (k + 2))$, $((m + 2^{n-k-2} + 2^{n-k-3}), (k + 3))$, etc., starting from the leftmost sibling.

Proof: Assume that the node number of v is $(a_1..a_k..a_n)$, which is m in decimal, where a_i is 0 or 1, $1 \leq i \leq k$. The node number of a child node of v, which is adjacent from v through v's down edge, is $(a_1..a_k 0 a_{k+2}..a_n)$ with $(k + 1)$ effective digits. The node numbers of v's other child nodes, of which each node is adjacent to its sibling through its sibling edge, are $(a_1..a_k 010..0_n)$, $(a_1..a_k 0110..0_n)$, etc. with $(k + 2)$, $(k + 3)$ effective digits, etc., respectively, which are $(m + 2^{n-k-2})$, $(m + 2^{n-k-2} + 2^{n-k-3})$, etc., respectively. Thus, when the node code of a node v is (m, k), node codes of v's child nodes are $(m, (k + 1))$, $((m + 2^{n-k-2}), (k + 2))$, $((m + 2^{n-k-2} + 2^{n-k-3}), (k + 2))$, etc. $\square$

From Remark 4, we maintain the nodecodes as decimal numbers and also keep effective digit information with each node. And, given two nodecodes for two nodes, we decide by arithmetic comparisons as to whether two nodes are connected.

7. Implementation of operators X^{Next}, $X^{Connected}$, and X^{Until}

In this section, we discuss the evaluation of temporal operators X^{Next}, $X^{Connected}$, and X^{Until}. For each operator, we give two algorithms, one that does use nodecodes, and another one that does not. We then compare the two alternatives by cost formulas. Please note that, in the *CO Pres_Nodes*, we have the adjacency list implementation of graphs (with the attributes *child-nodes* and *parent-nodes*).

We will use the following storage model for the *CO*'s and the evaluation of temporal operators. Let A be a *CO* with g_1, p_1, and possibly some other attributes, where g_1 contains the *oid*s of graph objects, and p_1 contains node *oid* sequences which represent paths. Let B be a *CO* with g_2, p_2, and possibly some other attributes, where g_2 contains graph *oid*s, and p_2 contains sequences of node *oid*s which represent paths. We assume that the main memory buffer *Buf* is of size b pages. The *CO A* is of size N pages, and each page holds t_{P_A} tuples. The *CO B* is of size M pages, and each page holds t_{P_B} tuples. The *CO Pres_Nodes* is of size T pages, and each page holds t_{P_N} tuples. For a given graph, there are P_A pages of A tuples and P_B pages of B tuples.

We make the assumption that, for a given graph with oid *goid*, $\sigma_{g_1=goid}(A) \cup \sigma_{g_2=goid}(B) \cup \sigma_{graph\_in=goid}(Pres\_Nodes)$ fits into the main memory buffer *Buf*; that is, $P_A + P_B + P_N < b - 1$. This is a reasonable assumption since presentation graphs are small, i.e., sparse graphs with less than 50 nodes.

7.1. Algorithms without using nodecodes

A. EvalNext algorithm. The procedure *EvalNext(A, B)* evaluates the O-Algebra operator $A \; X^{Next} \; B$, producing a new *CO* with a new attribute p. We assume that the *CO Pres_Nodes* is already sorted by graph *oid*'s.

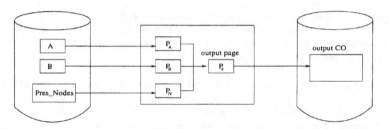

Figure 15.   Illustration of Step 2 of the algorithm EvalNext.

EvalNext(input A, B)
begin
  Sort A and B by graph oid's; { step 1: do **external merge-sort using the main memory**
  buffer Buf of b pages }
  for each graph g_i that appears both in A and B **do** { step 2: implement the operator X^{Next} }
    begin
      Read all P_A pages of graph g_i from A into buffer Buf; Call these pages partition P_1;
      Read all P_B pages of graph g_i from B into buffer Buf; Call these pages partition P_2;
      Read the $Pres\_Nodes$ pages of g_i into buffer Buf, and create an in-memory hash table
      with the hash key being the $graph\_in$ attribute; Call it P_3;
      for each tuple t_1 in P_1 **do**
        begin
          Fetch the $Pres\_Nodes$ tuple t_3 from P_3 by hashing such that $t_3.oid = Last(t_1.p_1)$;
          for each tuple t_2 in P_2 **do**
            if $Children(t_3)$ contains $First(t_2.p_2)$ **then**
              begin
                Create a tuple t from t_1 & t_2 and output into the "output page" P_4 in Buf;
                if P_4 is full **then** { P_4 is a single page }
                  Empty it by copying it to the disk as a page for the output CO;
              end
        end
    end
  Copy P_4 into the disk as the last page for the output CO;
end

Figure 16.   Algorithm EvalNext.

Cost Analysis of *EvalNext*:

Disk Accesses:

Step 1 sorts A, B, and *Pres_Nodes*. Here we use external merge sort. For A, In the
first pass, we read b pages at a time into buffer Buf and sort internally (for example, use
quicksort). In the following merge passes, we do a $(b-1)$-way merge (that is, use $(b-1)$
pages for input and use the remaining page for output). In each pass we read every page in
the file, process it, and write it out.

In Step 2, we check the *Next* relationship of A, B tuples for each graph. Since for a given graph, all the A, B, and *Pres_Nodes* tuples for that graph fit into the main memory buffer *Buf*, we only need to do a single scan of A, B and *Pres_Nodes* pages.

So the total number of disk accesses for *EvalNext* is:

Step 1: $2N(1 + \log_{b-1}\lceil \frac{N}{b}\rceil) + 2M(1 + \log_{b-1}\lceil \frac{M}{b}\rceil)$;
Step 2: $N + M + T$.

Number of Comparisons in *EvalNext*:

In Step 1, in the first pass of external merge sort on A, we break the entire file into $\lceil \frac{N}{b}\rceil$ subfiles of size b pages and sort internally, where each takes $c_1 \cdot b \cdot t_{P_A} \cdot \log(b \cdot t_{P_A})$ time. In the subsequent $(b-1)$-way merge passes, each pass makes $(b-2) \cdot N \cdot t_{P_A}$ comparisons.

In Step 2, for a graph g_i that appears both in A and B, for each A tuple t_1 of graph g_i, we scan all the tuples t_2 in B of that graph to check if they are adjacent to each other. That is, we have to get the tuple t_3 such that $t_3.oid = Last(t_1.p_1)$, and check if $First(t_2.p_2)$ is a member of t_3's *child-nodes* attribute. Assume that the number of *Children* elements in $Children(t_3)$ is k. Then the total number of comparisons for each graph g_i is $k \cdot P_A \cdot t_{P_A} \cdot P_B \cdot t_{P_B}$.

So the total number of comparisons is:

Step 1: $c_1 b t_{P_A} \log(b t_{P_A})\lceil \frac{N}{b}\rceil + \log_{b-1}\lceil \frac{N}{b}\rceil(b-2)Nt_{P_A}$ { for external merge sort of A }
   $+ c_1 b t_{P_B} \log(b t_{P_B})\lceil \frac{M}{b}\rceil + \log_{b-1}\lceil \frac{M}{b}\rceil(b-2)Mt_{P_B}$ { for external merge sort of B }
Step 2: for each iteration in the **for** loop:
   $P_A \cdot t_{P_A}$ { for fetching t_3 tuples }
   $+ k \cdot P_A \cdot t_{P_A} \cdot P_B \cdot t_{P_B}$ { for checking Next of t_1, t_2 }.

B. EvalConnected algorithm. The procedure *EvalConnected(A, B)*, given in figure 17, evaluates the O-Algebra operator $A\ X^{Connected}B$, producing a new CO with a new attribute p.

In *EvalConnected*, to check if $t_1.p_1$ is connected to $t_2.p_2$, we have to check each path p from "Begin" to "Terminate" in the graph. That is, for each path p, we check each node on p to see if $Last(t_1.p_1)$ appears on p, and if it is, we go on checking the following nodes to see if $First(t_2.p_2)$ appears.

Cost Analysis of *EvalConnected*:

Disk Accesses:

The total number of disk accesses is

Step 1: $2N(1 + \log_{b-1}\lceil \frac{N}{b}\rceil) + 2M(1 + \log_{b-1}\lceil \frac{M}{b}\rceil)$ { for external merge sort of A and B }
Step 2: $N + M + T$.

Number of Comparisons:

EvalConnected(input: A, B)
begin
  Sort A and B by graph *oids*; { step 1: use external merge-sort }
  for each graph g_i that appears both in A and B do { step 2: implement the operator $X^{Connected}$ }
    begin
      Read *Pres_Nodes* pages of graph g_i into buffer Buf;
      Compute the set of paths from the "Begin" node to the "Terminate" node for graph g_i and
      Create a tuple t for each path and output t to P_3;
      Read the A pages of graph g_i into buffer Buf; Call these pages partition P_1;
      Read the B pages of graph g_i into buffer Buf; Call these pages partition P_2;
      for each tuple t_1 in P_1 do
        for each tuple t_2 in P_2 do
          for each path tuple t_3 in P_3 do
            if $t_3.path$ contains Last($t_1.p_1$) (appearing first) & First($t_2.p_2$) (appearing later) then
            begin
              Create a tuple t from t_1, t_2 & t_3, and output t to P_4; { P_4 is a single page }
              if P_4 is full then
                Empty it by copying it to the disk as a page for the output CO;
            end
    end
  Copy P_4 into the disk as the last page for the output CO;
end

Figure 17.   Algorithm EvalConnected.

Step 1: $c_1 bt_{P_A} \log(bt_{P_A}) \lceil \frac{N}{b} \rceil + \log_{b-1} \lceil \frac{N}{b} \rceil (b-2) N t_{P_A}$ { for external merge sort of A }
          $+ c_1 bt_{P_B} \log(bt_{P_B}) \lceil \frac{M}{b} \rceil + \log_{b-1} \lceil \frac{M}{b} \rceil (b-2) M t_{P_B}$ { for external merge sort of B }
Step 2:   Let k_2 be the number of paths from "Begin" to "Terminate" in a graph. Then the
        number of comparisons for each iteration of the **for** loop is
        $P_N \cdot t_{P_N} + k \cdot P_N \cdot t_{P_N} + k_2$ { for computing paths from "Begin" to "Terminate" }
        $+ k_2 \cdot P_A \cdot t_{P_A} \cdot P_B \cdot t_{P_B}$ { for checking *Connected* } .

C. EvalUntil algorithm.   A simple algorithm for *EvalUntil* is described in figure 18.
$C = \sum_{j=1}^{i-1} C_i$ is the result CO for $A\ X^{Until}\ B$.

Cost Analysis of *EvalUntilBasic*:

    Let m be the maximum number of times p holds repetitively. Then the cost of *EvalUntil-Basic* is $m \cdot$ cost of *EvalNext*(A, B).

EvalUntilBasic(input A, B)
begin
    $C_1 =$ EvalNext(A, B);
    $i = 1$;
    while C_i is not Empty do
        begin
            $C_{i+1} =$ EvalNext(A, C_i)
            $i = i + 1$;
        end
    end

Figure 18.   Algorithm EvalUntilBasic.

```
EvalUntil(input A, B)
begin
    Sort A and B by graph oid's; { step 1: use external merge sort }
    for each graph gᵢ that appears both in A and B do { step 2: implement the operator X^Until }
        begin
            Read all Pₐ pages of graph gᵢ from A into buffer Buf; Call these pages partition P₁;
            Read all P_B pages of graph gᵢ from B into buffer Buf; Call these pages partition P₂;
            Read the Pres_Nodes pages of gᵢ into buffer Buf, and create an in-memory hash table
                with the hash key being the graph_in attribute; Call it P₃;
            while P₂ is not empty do
                begin
                    for each tuple t₁ in P₁ do
                        begin
                            Fetch the Pres_Node tuple t₃ from P₃ by hashing such that t₃.oid = Last(t₁.p₁);
                            for each tuple t₂ in P₂ do
                                if Children(t₃) contains First(t₂.p₂) then
                                    begin
                                        Create a tuple t from t₁ & t₂ and output into the "output page" P₄ in Buf;
                                        if P₄ is full then { P₄ is a single page }
                                            Empty it by copying it into the disk as a page for (a) the output
                                            CO, and (b) the Temp CO;
                                    end
                        end
                    Empty P₄ by copying it into the disk as a page for (a) the ouput CO, and (b) Temp CO;
                    Read all Temp pages from disk into buffer Buf as the "new" P₂ partition;
                end
        end
end
```

Figure 19. Algorithm EvalUntil.

We can improve the algorithm in figure 18 by repetitively evaluating *Next* (and thus *Until*) on a graph-by-graph basis. The algorithm in figure 19 illustrates the improvement.

Cost Analysis of *EvalUntil*:

Disk Accesses:

Step 1: $2N(1 + \log_{b-1} \lceil \frac{N}{b} \rceil) + 2M(1 + \log_{b-1} \lceil \frac{M}{b} \rceil)$; { for external merge sort of A, B }

In Step 2, in addition to a single scan of A, B and $Pres\_Node$ pages, we have to load the pages of Temp CO, which is of the same size as the output CO. Assume that the size of the output CO is R pages, then the number of disk accesses is

Step 2: $N + M + T + R$.

Number of Comparisons in *EvalUntil*:

Step 1: $c_1 bt_{P_A} \log(bt_{P_A}) \lceil \frac{N}{b} \rceil + \log_{b-1} \lceil \frac{N}{b} \rceil (b-2)Nt_{P_A}$ { for external merge sort of A }
$+ c_1 bt_{P_B} \log(bt_{P_B}) \lceil \frac{M}{b} \rceil + \log_{b-1} \lceil \frac{M}{b} \rceil (b-2)Mt_{P_B}$ { for external merge sort of B }

Step 2: for each iteration in the **for** loop:
$P_A \cdot t_{P_A} \cdot m$ { for fetching t_3 tuples }
$+ m \cdot k \cdot P_A \cdot t_{P_A} \cdot k_5$ { for checking Next of t_1, t_2 }.

Here, m is the maximum number of times p holds repetitively, and k_5 is the average number of tuples in partition P_2 at each iteration.

7.2. Algorithms with nodecodes

We now make the assumption that each of the attributes p_1 in A and p_2 in B contains a set of nodecode pairs, where all pairs denote the same path.[4] Please note that a path p in a graph can be uniquely specified by only keeping the nodecodes of the first and the last node of p. Since a node may have multiple nodecodes, a path may have multiple pairs of nodecodes for the same begin and end node.

The main memory buffer *Buf* is of size b pages. The *CO A* is of size N' pages, and each page holds t'_{P_A} tuples. The *CO B* is of size M' pages, and each page holds t'_{P_B} tuples. The *CO Pres_Nodes* is of size T pages, and each page holds t_{P_N} tuples. For a given graph, there are P'_A pages of A tuples and P'_B pages of B tuples.

Again we make the assumption that, for a given graph with oid *goid*, $\sigma_{g_1=goid}(A) \cup \sigma_{g_2=goid}(B) \cup \sigma_{graph\_in=goid}(Pres\_Nodes)$ fits into the main memory buffer *Buf*; that is, $P'_A + P'_B + P_N < b - 1$.

A. EvalNextNodecodes algorithm. With nodecodes, a path is uniquely represented by the pair of nodecodes of the first and last node of the path. In *EvalNextNodecodes*, to check whether $t_1.p_1$ is next to $t_2.p_2$, we only need to compare the nodecode of $t_1.p_1$'s last node (say e_1) with the nodecode of $t_2.p_2$'s first node (say b_2). If e_1 is a prefix of b_2, then $t_1.p_1$ is next to $t_2.p_2$. Since each path has multiple pairs of nodecodes where each pair corresponds to a distinct path from the "Begin" node of the graph to the path, we have to compare each pair of nodecodes for t_1 and t_2. Thus, in the p attribute of the result tuple t, for each distinct path from the graph's "Begin" node to the path combined from t_1 and t_2, the corresponding nodecode pair is a member of p.

Cost Analysis of *EvalNextNodecodes*:

Disk Accesses:

Step 1: $2N'(1 + \log_{b-1} \lceil \frac{N'}{b} \rceil) + 2M'(1 + \log_{b-1} \lceil \frac{M'}{b} \rceil)$ { for external merge sort of A and B }
Step 2: $N' + M'$

Number of Comparisons:

Step 1: $c_1 b t'_{P_A} \log(b t'_{P_A}) \lceil \frac{N'}{b} \rceil + \log_{b-1} \lceil \frac{N'}{b} \rceil (b-2)N' t'_{P_A}$ { for external merge sort of A}
$+ c_1 b t'_{P_B} \log(b t'_{P_B}) \lceil \frac{M'}{b} \rceil + \log_{b-1} \lceil \frac{M'}{b} \rceil (b-2)M' t'_{P_B}$ { for external merge sort of B }
Step 2: number of comparisons for each iteration in the **for** loop:
$P'_A \cdot t'_{P_A} \cdot k_3 \cdot P'_B \cdot t'_{P_A} \cdot k_4$ { for checking *Next* }

EvalNextNodecodes(input A, B)
begin
  Sort A and B by graph *oids*; {step 1: use external merge sort }
  for each graph g_i that appears both in A and B do { step 2: implement the operator X^{Next} }
    begin
      Read the A pages of graph g_i into buffer; Call these pages partition P_1;
      Read the B pages of graph g_i into buffer; Call these pages partition P_2;
      for each tuple t_1 in P_1 do
        for each tuple t_2 in P_2 do
          if $t_1.p_1$ is *Next* to $t_2.p_2$ **then** { there exists $< b_1, e_1 >$ in $t_1.p_1$ and $< b_2, e_2 >$
                       in $t_2.p_2$ such that $b_2 = e_1 01^*$ }
           begin
             Create a tuple t from t_1, t_2, and output t to P_4; { P_4 is a single page }
             { for each $< b_1, e_1 >$ in $t_1.p_1$, $< b_2, e_2 >$ in $t_2.p_2$, if $b_2 = e_1 01^*$, $< b_1, e_2 >$
             will be a member of $t.p$. }
             if P_4 is full **then**
                Empty it by copying it to the disk as a page for the output CO;
           end
    end
  Copy P_4 into the disk as the last page for the output CO;
end

Figure 20.   Algorithm EvalNextNodeCodes.

Here, k_3 is the average number of nodecode pairs in the p_1 attribute of an A tuple, and k_4 is the average number of nodecode pairs in the p_2 attribute of a B tuple.

B. EvalConnectedNodecodes algorithm.   In *EvalConnectedNodecodes*, to check if $t_1.p_1$ is connected to $t_2.p_2$, we only need to compare the nodecode of $t_1.p_1$'s last node (say e_1) with $t_2.p_2$'s first node (say b_2). If $b_2 = e_1(01^*)^+$, then they are connected. Again, since each path has multiple pairs of nodecodes where each corresponds to a different path from the "Begin" node of the graph to the path, we have to compare each pair of nodecodes for t_1 and t_2.

Cost Analysis of *EvalConnectedNodecodes*:

Disk Access:

Step 1: $2N'(1 + \log_{b-1} \lceil \frac{N'}{b} \rceil) + 2M'(1 + \log_{b-1} \lceil \frac{M'}{b} \rceil)$ { for external merge sort of A
      and B }
Step 2: $N' + M'$

Number of Comparisons:

Step 1: $c_1 bt'_{P_A} \log(bt'_{P_A}) \lceil \frac{N'}{b} \rceil + \log_{b-1} \lceil \frac{N'}{b} \rceil (b-2)N't'_{P_A}$ { for external merge sort of A }
      $+ c_1 bt'_{P_B} \log(bt'_{P_B}) \lceil \frac{M'}{b} \rceil + \log_{b-1} \lceil \frac{M'}{b} \rceil (b-2)M't'_{P_B}$ { for external merge sort
      of B }
Step 2: number of comparisons for each iteration in the **for** loop:
      $P'_A \cdot t'_{P_A} \cdot k_3 \cdot P'_B \cdot t'_{P_B} \cdot k_4$ { for checking *Connected* }

EvalConnectedNodecodes(input: A, B)
begin
    Sort A, B by graph *oids*; { step 1: external merge sort of A, B }
    for each graph g_i that appears both in A and B **do** { step 2: implement the operator $X^{Connected}$ }
      begin
        Read the A pages of graph g_i into buffer; Call these pages partition P_1;
        Read the B pages of graph g_i into buffer; Call these pages partition P_2;
        for each tuple t_1 in P_1 **do**
          for each tuple t_2 in P_2 **do**
            if $t_2.p_2$ is *Connected* to $t_1.p_1$ **then** {there exist $< b_1, e_1 >$ in $t_1.p_1$ and $< b_2, e_2 >$
               in $t_2.p_2$ such that $b_2 = e_1(01^*)^+$ }
            begin
              Create a tuple t from t_1 & t_2 and output t to P_4; { P_4 is a single page }
              { for each $< b_1, e_1 >$ in $t_1.p_1$, $< b_2, e_2 >$ in $t_2.p_2$, if $b_2 = e_1(01^*)^+$, $< b_1, e_2 >$
              will be a member of $t.p.$ }
              if P_4 is full **then**
                Empty it by copying it to the disk as a page for the output CO;
            end
      end
    Copy P_4 into the disk as the last page for the output CO;
end

Figure 21.   Algorithm EvalConnectedNodecodes.

Here, k_3 is the average number of nodecode pairs in the p_1 attribute of an A tuple, and k_4 is the average number of nodecode pairs in the p_2 attribute of a B tuple.

C. *EvalUntilNodecodes* algorithm.   We now give the algorithm for *EvalUntilNodecodes*. The basic approach is identical to the algorithm in figure 18.

Cost Analysis of *EvalUntilNodecodesBasic*: $m \cdot$ the cost of *EvalNextNodecodes*(A, B).

And, revising the algorithm in figure 22 so that *Until* is completely evaluated on a graph-by-graph basis, we have the algorithm in figure 23.

Cost Analysis of *EvalUntilNodecodes*:

Disk Accesses:

Step 1: $2N'(1 + \log_{b-1} \lceil \frac{N'}{b} \rceil) + 2M'(1 + \log_{b-1} \lceil \frac{M'}{b} \rceil)$ { for external merge sort of A
      and B }

Let the size of the output CO be R' pages. Again, in Step 2, in addition to a single file scan of A and B, we need to load the pages of Temp CO, which is of the same size as the output CO. So the number of disk accesses is

Step 2: $N' + M' + R'$

Number of Comparisons:

```
EvalUntilNodeCodesBasic(input A, B)
begin
    C₁ = EvalNextNodecodes(A, B);
    i = 1;
    while Cᵢ is not Empty do
        begin
            Cᵢ₊₁ = EvalNextNodecodes(A, Cᵢ)
            i = i + 1;
        end
end
```

Figure 22. Algorithm EvalUntilNodecodesBasic.

```
EvalUntilNodecodes(input A, B)
begin
    Sort A and B by graph oids; {step 1: use external merge sort }
    for each graph gᵢ that appears both in A and B do { step 2: implement the operator X^Until }
    begin
        Read the A pages of graph gᵢ into buffer; Call these pages partition P₁;
        Read the B pages of graph gᵢ into buffer; Call these pages partition P₂;
        while P₂ is not empty do
            begin
                for each tuple t₁ in P₁ do
                    for each tuple t₂ in P₂ do
                        if t₁.p₁ is Next to t₂.p₂ then { there exists < b₁, e₁ > in t₁.p₁ and < b₂, e₂ >
                                                       in t₂.p₂ such that b₂ = e₁01* }
                        begin
                            Create a tuple t from t₁, t₂, and output t to P₄; { P₄ is a single page }
                            { for each < b₁, e₁ > in t₁.p₁, < b₂, e₂ > in t₂.p₂, if b₂ = e₁01*,
                            < b₁, e₂ > will be a member of t.path.}
                            if P₄ is full then
                                Empty it by copying it into the disk as a page for (a) the output CO,
                                and (b) the Temp CO;
                        end
                    Empty P₄ by copying it into the disk as a page for (a) the output CO, and (b) Temp CO;
                    Read all Temp pages from disk into buffer Buf as the "new" P₂ partition;
            end
    end
end
```

Figure 23. Algorithm EvalUntilNodecodes.

Step 1: $c_1 bt'_{P_A} \log(bt'_{P_A}) \lceil \frac{N'}{b} \rceil + \log_{b-1} \lceil \frac{N'}{b} \rceil (b-2)N' t'_{P_A}$ { for external merge sort of A }
$+ c_1 bt'_{P_B} \log(bt'_{P_B}) \lceil \frac{M'}{b} \rceil + \log_{b-1} \lceil \frac{M'}{b} \rceil (b-2)M' t'_{P_B}$ { for external merge sort of B }

Step 2: number of comparisons for each iteration in the **for** loop:
$m \cdot P'_A \cdot t'_{P_A} \cdot k_3 \cdot k_4 \cdot k_5$ { for checking *Next* }

Here, m is the maximum number of times p holds repetitively; k_3 is the average number of nodecode pairs in the p_1 attribute of an A tuple; k_4 is the average number of nodecode pairs in the path attribute of a tuple in partition P_2; and k_5 is the average number of tuples in partition P_2 at each iteration.

87

7.3. Preliminary comparisons

In Sections 7.1 and 7.2, we have given two algorithms for each temporal operator, one that uses nodecodes, and one that does not. All six algorithms are coded into GVISUAL query processing; however, we have not yet empirically evaluated these algorithms with extensive runs. Nevertheless, by using the cost formulas derived for each operator, we can make several observations.

Observation 1.   For each temporal operator, the evaluation algorithm with nodecodes always has smaller number of disk accesses than the evaluation algorithm without nodecodes.

   Observation 1 follows from the fact that nodecode-based algorithms do not need to load the pages of the *Pres_Nodes CO*.

Observation 2.   For each temporal operator, the evaluation algorithm with nodecodes uses smaller number of camparisons than the evaluation algorithm without nodecodes.

   For Observation 2, we can make the assumption that, approximately, $P_A = P'_A$, $P_B = P'_B$, $t_{P_A} = t'_{P_A}$, $t_{P_B} = t'_{P_B}$, $N = N'$, $M = M'$. Then, it is clear that, in each iteration of the **for** loop of each operator, nodecode-based algorithms have much less comparisons. The improvement is especially notable for the *Connected* operator. The algorithm with nodecodes evaluates the *Connected* operator by making nodecode comparisons on the end points of the paths being checked; thus the costly graph traversal is eliminated. So overall, for each operator, the algorithm with *nodecodes* is more efficient than the one without nodecodes.

   There are also drawbacks for the *nodecode* system. It has the graph traversal overhead in assigning the *nodecodes*, as well as the transformation need between the two representations of paths, that is, the paths represented by sequences of node *oids* and the paths represented by pairs of nodecodes. Also, in the case of graph updates, the maintenance of the *nodecodes* may be costly.

8.   ViSiOn

ViSiOn is an object-oriented distributed database management system with a graphical user interface and an efficient object storage and retrieval mechanism for multimedia databases. ViSiOn utilizes the client server methodology in its architecture (see figure 24).

   The client portion of ViSiOn (ViSiOn client) contains two major components. Presentation Manager is the user's access point to the system. Presentation Manager communicates with Client Scheduler (for presentation scheduling and presentation data). The second major component of the ViSiOn client is GVISUAL. GVISUAL is the user interface for querying multimedia information as well as conventional data. There are three different servers in ViSiOn. The first server is the Disk server, which stores and retrieves the objects to and from the physical disks. Disk servers are capable of delivering multimedia streams. The control of data flow between the server and client is crucial when jitter free presentations of multimedia is desired. For this reason, Disk Servers contain a component called Client Scheduler. The Client Scheduler controls the data flow between ViSiOn clients and the Disk server. The second type of servers are VStore servers. VStore servers execute GVISUAL queries using

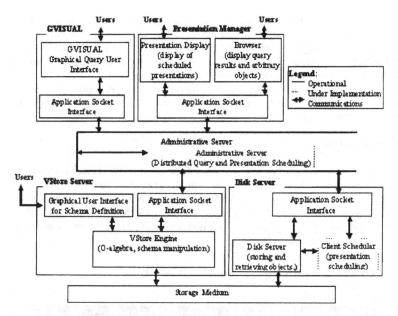

Figure 24. ViSiOn architecture.

O-algebra operators. Disk servers and VStore servers are multi-threaded applications. The last kind of server is the ViSiOn Administrative Server. This server holds the information neccessary to distribute queries and presentation requests among the ViSiOn servers.

9. Related work

To model the interactions between different types of multimedia data in a given multimedia presentation, many multimedia synchronization models are proposed in the literature [6, 12, 29]. Most of these models are graph- and constraint-based, utilizing directed acyclic graphs or variants of petrinets. The most powerful authoring tools such as Authorware [22] (http://www.macrome-dia.com), IconAuthor [15] (http://www.aimtech.com), and Quest [26] (http://www.allencomm.com) use (with quite different user interfaces) presentation graphs (or flowcharts) with icons and thumbnails (representing multimedia data) as nodes, and edges for synchronization. Recently, some commercial multimedia authoring tools have announced the use of databases. However, to the best of our knowledge, the interaction between a multimedia authoring tool and a multimedia database is loose, and the database is used for only very basic purposes.

We have also designed and implemented prototype multimedia authoring tools for construction of presentation graphs [23, 27]. Both tools use drag-and-drop icons, dialog boxes, etc., to build multimedia presentations and store them into a multimedia database.

A work that has similarities to GVISUAL is reported by Sistla et al. [28], which proposes a calculus-based language, Hierarchical Temporal Logic (HTL), for specifying queries on video data. Like GVISUAL, HTL deals with specifying composition hierarchy of video data, e.g., a segment consisting of several sub-segments, and sequence of segments at the same level of the composition hierarchy. HTL uses predicates (for example, the predicate **at-shot-level**(g) asserts that g is satisfied at the shot level) and operators **next** and **until** to specify the composition hierarchy and the sequence, respectively.

CHIMP [8, 30] is a multimedia authoring and presentation system that deals with authoring, retrieval and scheduling of presentations. However, CHIMP does not deal with the querying of presentations.

10. Conclusions

In this paper, we have given the query processing algorithms for GVISUAL, a graphical language for querying multimedia presentations. The algorithms have been implemented, and GVISUAL is functional. However, we have not yet performed extensive performance evaluation tests on either GVISUAL or the implementation algorithms described in Section 7, which is future work. Another research area is optimizing O-Algebra expressions that involve path algebra operators.

Appendix A. Actual parse trees generated by GVISUAL

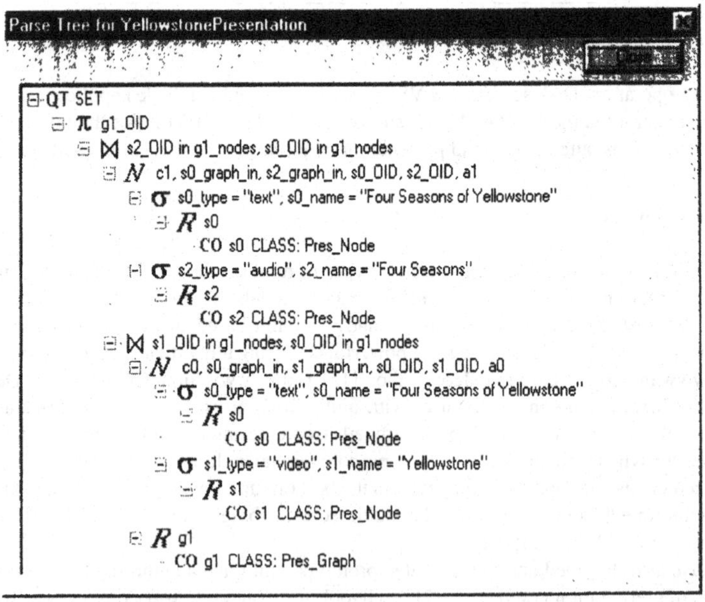

Parse Tree for YellowstonePresentation

```
⊟-QT SET
   ⊟ π g1_OID
      ⊟ ⋈ s2_OID in g1_nodes, s0_OID in g1_nodes
         ⊟ N c1, s0_graph_in, s2_graph_in, s0_OID, s2_OID, a1
            ⊟ σ s0_type = "text", s0_name = "Four Seasons of Yellowstone"
               ⊟ R s0
                  CO s0 CLASS: Pres_Node
            ⊟ σ s2_type = "audio", s2_name = "Four Seasons"
               ⊟ R s2
                  CO s2 CLASS: Pres_Node
      ⊟ ⋈ s1_OID in g1_nodes, s0_OID in g1_nodes
         ⊟ N c0, s0_graph_in, s1_graph_in, s0_OID, s1_OID, a0
            ⊟ σ s0_type = "text", s0_name = "Four Seasons of Yellowstone"
               ⊟ R s0
                  CO s0 CLASS: Pres_Node
            ⊟ σ s1_type = "video", s1_name = "Yellowstone"
               ⊟ R s1
                  CO s1 CLASS: Pres_Node
      ⊟ R g1
         CO g1 CLASS: Pres_Graph
```

Figure A1.   Full parse tree of the GVISUAL query YellowstonePresentation (in figure 5).

90

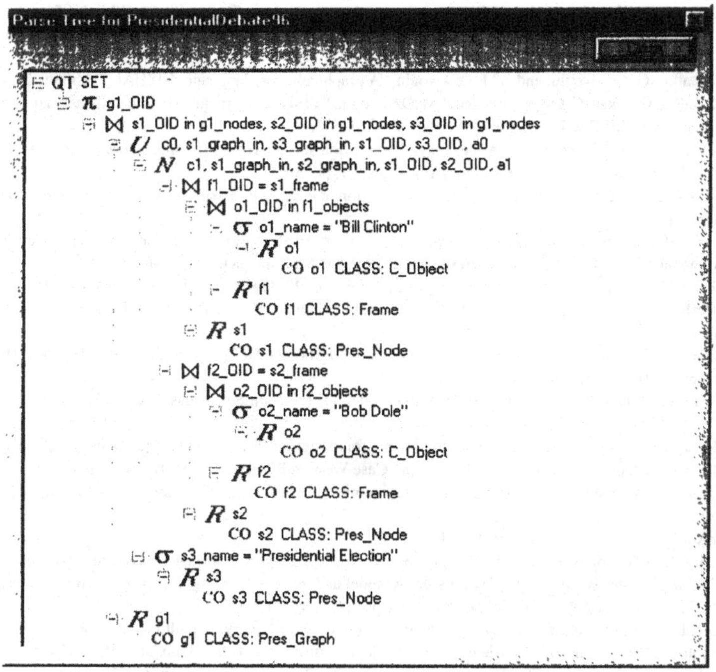

Figure A2. Full parse tree of the GVISUAL query PresidentialDebates96 (in figure 12).

Acknowledgment

This research is supported by the National Science Foundation Grants IRI 96-31214 and CDA 95-29503.

Notes

1. Note that the description is minimal and only for the explanation of the structure of a presentation graph.
2. A number of frames, called *representative frames*, from a stream are selected to model and represent content-based objects and content-based relationships for that stream. The selection of representative frames are done by domain experts.
3. The begin node with no incoming edges is called a *source node*. The terminate node with no outgoing edges is called a *sink node*.
4. Please note that this assumption introduces a maximum of two levels of nesting in *CO*s, as compared to the previous rule of *at most one level of nesting of COs*.

References

1. A. Al-Hamdani, "Implementing GVISUAL for multimedia presentation querying," M.S. Thesis, CWRU, June 1998.

2. N.H. Balkir, "VISUAL: a graphical icon-based query language," M.S. Thesis, CWRU, May 1995.
3. N.H. Balkir and G. Ozsoyoglu, "Buffer management for continuous delivery of presentation graphs," in 4th Int. Workshop on Multimedia DBMS, August 1998.
4. N.H. Balkir, G. Ozsoyoglu, and Z.M. Ozsoyoglu, "A graphical query language: VISUAL," submitted.
5. N.H. Balkir, E. Sukan, G. Ozsoyoglu, and Z.M. Ozsoyoglu, "VISUAL: a graphical icon-based query language," in Proceedings, IEEE ICDE Conference, 1996, pp. 524–533.
6. G. Blakowski and R. Steinmetz, "A media synchronization survey: reference model, specification, and case studies," IEEE J. on Sel. Areas in Comm., Vol. 14, No. 1, pp. 5–35, 1996.
7. T. Bozkaya, N.H. Balkir, and T. Lee, "Efficient evaluation of path algebra expressions," Tech. Report, CWRU, November 1997.
8. K.S. Candan, B. Prabhakaran, and V.S. Subramanian, "CHIMP: a framework for supporting distributed multimedia document authoring and presentation," in ACM Multimedia Conf., 1996.
9. R.G.G. Cattell (Ed.), The Object Database Standard: ODMG-93, Morgan Kaufmann Publishers, 1993.
10. V. Deshpande and P. Larson, "An algebra for nested relations," Tech. Report, University of Waterloo, 1987.
11. E. Emerson, "Temporal and modal logic," in Handbook of Theoretical Computer Science, J. Leeuwen (Ed.), Elsevier, 1990, pp. 995–1072, Ch. 16.
12. M. Haindl, "A new multimedia synchronization model," IEEE J. on Sel. Areas in Comm., Vol. 14, No. 1, pp. 73–83, 1996.
13. V. Hakkoymaz, "A constraint-driven methodology for designing a multimedia presentation system from multimedia databases," Ph.D. Thesis, CES Dept., Case Western Reserve University, December 1996.
14. D. Huffman "A method for the construction of minimum-redundancy codes," Proceedings of the IRE, Vol. 40, No. 9, 1952.
15. IconAuthor User Manual, AimTech Inc., June 1997.
16. W. Kim, Introduction to Object-Oriented Databases, The MIT Press: Cambridge, Massachusetts, 1990.
17. H.C. Kuo, "A rule-based cooperative transaction model and event processing in real-time active databases," Ph.D. Thesis, CES Dept., Case Western Reserve University, May 1997.
18. T. Lee, L. Sheng, T. Bozkaya, G. Ozsoyoglu, and M. Ozsoyoglu, "Querying multimedia presentations based on content," IEEE Trans. on Knowledge and Data Engineering, Vol. 11, No. 3, pp. 361–385, 1999.
19. J. Lin and Z.M. Ozsoyoglu, "Processing OODB queries by O-Algebra," in Proc. of CIKM, 1996.
20. J. Lin, X. Zhang and Z.M. Ozsoyoglu, "A complete solution of reducing OODB nested queries," Tech. Report, CWRU, 1997.
21. T.D.C. Little, and A. Ghafoor, "Synchronization and storage models for multimedia objects," IEEE Jour. on Selected Areas of Communications, Vol. 8, No. 3, pp. 413–427, 1990.
22. Macromedia AuthorWare 4: Using Authorware, Macromedia Inc, 1997.
23. R. Ortega, "Design and implementation of a video presentation tool," M.S. Project, CWRU, May 1997.
24. G. Ozsoyoglu and H. Wang, "A relational calculus with set operators, its safety, and equivalent graphical languages," IEEE Trans. on Software Engineering, Vol. 15, No. 9, pp. 1038–1052, September 1989.
25. B. Prabhakaran, Multimedia Database Management Systems, Kluwer Academic Publishers, 1996.
26. Quest User's Guide, Allen Communication Inc., May 1996.
27. K. Renganathan, "A presentation authoring tool," M.S. Project, CWRU, October 1997.
28. A.P. Sistla, C. Yu, and R. Venkatasubrahmanian, "Similarity based retrieval of videos," in Proceedings, IEEE ICDE Conference, 1997, pp. 181–190.
29. R. Steinmetz "Synchronization properties on multimedia systems," IEEE J. on Sel. Areas in Comm., Vol. 8, No. 3, pp. 401–412, 1990.
30. V.S. Subramanian., Principles of Multimedia Database Systems, Morgan Kaufman Publishers, 1998.
31. R. Taylor, "Design and implementation of a multimedia application using IconAuthor," M.S. Project, May 1998.
32. J. Widom and S. Ceri, Active Database Systems, Morgan Kaufman Publishers, 1997.
33. P. Wolper, "Temporal logic can be more expressive," in IEEE Symposium on Foundations of Computer Science, 1981, pp. 340–348.

Taekyong Lee received the bachelor degree in economics from the Korea University, the Master degree in economics from the Indiana University, Bloomington and the Ph.D. degree from the case Western Reserve University in computer science in 1998. Taekyong Lee is presently a tenured lecturer at Kyungsan University, Korea. His research interests include multimedia databases, knowledgebase systems, data mining and artificial intelligence.

Lei Sheng received a B.S. degree in Computer Science from Fudan University, China in 1991 and M.E. degree in Computer Engineering and Science from Zhejiang University, China in 1994. Currently she is a Ph.D. student in Computer Science at Case Western Reserve University. Her research interests include database query languages, object oriented databases and multimedia databases.

Nevzat Hurkan Balkir has recently finished his Ph.D. degree in the Computer Engineering and Science Department, Case Western Reserve University. He received his M.S. degree from Case Western Reserve University, and his B.Sc. degree from Bilkent University, Ankara, Turkey in 1995 and 1993, respectively. N.H. Balkir's primary research interests are in the areas of object oriented databases, multimedia databases and multimedia computing.

Abdullah Al-Hamdani is a Ph.D. student in the Computer Science program, Electrical Engineering and Computer Science department, Case Western Reserve University. He received his B.Sc. degree (1995) in Computer Science from Sultan Qaboos University, Oman, and M.Sc. Degree (1998) in Computer Science from Case Western Reserve University. His areas of interest include databases and web computing.

Gultekin Ozsoyoglu is a Professor of the Department of Computer Engineering and Science, Case Western Reserve University, Cleveland, Ohio. He received his Ph.D. degree in Computing Science from the University of Alberta, Edmonton, Alberta, Canada, in 1980. G. Ozsoyoglu's current research interests include multimedia databases, electronic books and Web databases, scientific and statistical databases and graphical user interfaces. Dr. Ozsoyoglu has published in all of the major database conferences and journals such as ACM Transactions on Database Systems, IEEE Transactions on Software Engineering, IEEE Transactions on Knowledge and Data Engineering, and Journal of Computer and System Sciences. He has served in program committees and panels of major database conferences such as ACM SIGMOD, VLDB, IEEE Data Engineering. He was an ACM national lecturer, general chair of the 11th Scientific and Statistical Database Conference, program chair of 3rd Statistical and Scientific Database Conference, workshops general chair of the CIKM'94 and CIKM'96 Conferences, Research Prototypes chair of ACM SIGMOD'94 conference, and a guest editor for IEEE Transactions on Knowledge and Data Engineering. He is an associate editor of the Journal of Database Administration, and has served of NSF, NRC, and Ford Foundation panels.

Z. Meral Ozsoyoglu has a B.Sc. degree in Electrical Engineering, and a M.Sc. degree in Computer Science, both from Middle East Technical University, Turkey. She has a Ph.D. degree in Computer Science from the University of Alberta, Canada. She is a Professor of Computer Engineering and Science at Case Western Reserve University, where she has been a faculty member since 1980. Z. Meral Ozsoyoglu's primary research work and interests are in the areas of principles of database systems, database query languages, database design, object oriented databases and complex objects with applications in scientific, temporal, and multimedia databases. She has published several papers on these topics in computer science journals and conferences. She was ACM PODS Program chair in 1997, and has served on organizing and program committees of several major conferences on databases. She has been a recipient of several NSF grants as well as an IBM Faculty Development Award, and an NSF FAW award. She is presently ACM SIGMOD Vice Chair.

Design of Multi-User Editing Servers for Continuous Media

SHAHRAM GHANDEHARIZADEH   shahram@cs.usc.edu
SEON HO KIM   seonkim@cs.usc.edu
Department of Computer Science, University of Southern California, Los Angeles, CA 90089, USA

Abstract. Based on a fifteen month investigation of a post production facilities for both the entertainment industry and broadcasters, we identified a number of challenges with the design and implementation of a server in support of multiple editing stations. These include, how to: share the same content among multiple editors, support continuous display of the edited content for each editor, support complex editing operations, compute the set of changes (deltas) proposed by an editor, compare the deltas proposed by multiple editors, etc. It is beyond the focus of this paper to report on each challenge and its related solutions. Instead, we focus on one challenge, namely how to support continuous display of the edited content for each editors, and techniques for physical organization of data to address this challenge.

Keywords: nonlinear editing, buffering, data placement, continuous media

1. Introduction

Video editing systems have been around for several decades now. They are used extensively by the content providers, e.g., the entertainment industry, broadcasters, etc. Over time and with technical advances, they have evolved to utilize different storage mediums. The original mechanical devises, named Moviola, manipulated film (a positive print and NOT the negative itself). The mid 1970s witnessed editing systems based on analog tape. In the 1990s, editing systems that employed digital tape and magnetic disks became common place. The tape-based systems are termed *linear* editing systems because they incurs a noticeable latency when a user manipulates content stored in a noncontiguous manner. The disk-based systems are termed *nonlinear* editing systems because they can quickly re-position the disk head to a new cylinder without scanning all cylinders, resulting in a lower latency when the user jumps from one video segment to another.

Linear editing systems are appropriate for small operations where a few editors work on different projects. They become inefficient for large projects with tight deadlines that require the collaboration of several editors. To illustrate and without loss of generality, we focus on one application from the entertainment industry, namely, the advertisement departments of major studios in Hollywood. (The requirements of this department are similar to other applications in both the entertainment and broadcasting industries.) The advertisement departments are required to generate 30 to 60 second trailers in a short period of time. The original version of the movie might be anywhere from 20 to 40 hours long.[1] The previewing of this content requires more than a day. At times, the deadlines are so tight,[2] that an executive decision is made to partition the work among multiple editors.

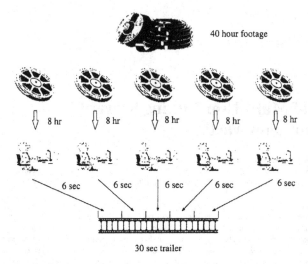

Figure 1. An example of cooperation among editors.

For example, with five editors and a 30 second trailer, the 40 hour footage is shown once to all the editors. Next, each editor is assigned an 8 hour segment and asked to contribute 6 seconds worth of material to the final trailer (see figure 1). Obviously, the flow of content in the resulting trailer depends on how closely the editors collaborate, communicate, and share their content with one another. With extremely tight deadlines, the 40 hour previewing step might be eliminated all together. Typically, this results in trailers that do not hint at a story line; instead, they are action packed segments. This might also happen when editors fail to collaborate closely when authoring their 6 second segment (even when the editors are provided with a preview of the 40 hour footage).

With servers in support of nonlinear editing stations, content can be shared among multiple editors in support of an effective collaboration paradigm. This paradigm empowers several editors to share the 40 hour footage, preview each other's (in progress) work, and make decisions that improve the quality of the final content. With relaxed deadlines, multiple editors can introduce different trailers that are readily available for previewing. In this case, it is desirable to have additional capabilities to reason about the set of changes proposed by each editor (deltas [6]), the difference between two or more deltas, and how to combine aspects of different deltas in order to introduce a new trailer.

This environment can be compared with a client-server software development environment that consists of workstations connected to a file server. The latency for sequentially browsing a file (video) should be less than 100 milliseconds [3]. Similarly, jumping from one line (frame) of the file (video) to another and referencing different files (video clips) should not be noticeable. The client-server nature should not impact the correctness or behavior of a program (previewing of an edited clip). Otherwise, it is difficult to determine whether the program (edited clip) or the system is at fault. To elaborate further, editors are artists who pay attention to details. Once they introduce a special effect and request the system to display the edited clip, they do not want to incur *system hiccups* (disruptions and delays caused by either the disk subsystem or the client-server architecture). This is because a hiccup might be interpreted as a side-effect of their work. This study investigates the physical design of data in support of a hiccup-free display in nonlinear editing servers.

For the purpose of this study, it is worthwhile to differentiate between two kinds of presentations: linear and nonlinear. With a linear presentation, the order of display is identical to the order of original data stored on the disk drives. For example, if video frames in a clip are stored as A, B, C, D, then a linear presentation of the clip entails a sequential retrieval and display of these frames (figure 2(a)). However, with a nonlinear presentation, the order of display can be different from the order of storage. Moreover, there could be multiple ways of ordering data for different presentations (figure 2(b)). A nonlinear editing server should support displays whose frames are stored in an arbitrary order (logical display orders). Changing the storage order (physical order) or duplicating data is not appropriate due to the noticeable latency incurred by the transfer of large volume of data. To support frame level nonlinear editing, each frame should be uniquely identified in the system. The entertainment industry employs a standard SMPTE timecode (*hour:minute:second:frame*) [15] for this purpose.

Due to the large size of continuous media, transmission of data is based on a just-in-time schedule: data is retrieved from disks and transmitted to the display in a timely manner that prevents hiccups. A cycle-based data retrieval technique [11, 16, 22] is one such approach. We describe this technique with a running example. Assume a video clip A with 4Mb/s of bandwidth requirement is partitioned into equi-sized blocks of 512KB. The time to display a block is termed a *time period* and denoted as $T_p = B/R_C$, where B is the size of a block and R_C is the bandwidth requirement of a continuous media type. In our example, a time period is one second long. Assuming constant-bit-rate (CBR) media, when A (starting with A_i) is referenced, the system retrieves A_i and initiates its display. Prior to completion of a time period (its display), it initiates the retrieval of A_{i+1} in order to ensure a continuous display. This process is repeated in a cyclic manner until all blocks of A have been displayed. If the time to retrieve a block, termed *block retrieval time*, is smaller than or equal to the time period then the display will be hiccup free. The time duration between the arrival of a request for A and the start of A_i's display is termed *startup latency*.

Using the concepts from both cycle-based and deadline-driven scheduling techniques, this study proposes data placement, buffering, and scheduling techniques in support of multi-user editing servers for continuous media. First, in Section 2, we investigate alternative retrieval techniques for a single disk system and propose a hybrid technique between frame and block based retrieval. By comparing round-robin and random placement, we determine random placement as the choice of data placement technique across multiple disk drives because random provides a shorter startup latency. However, random might introduce hiccups due to the variance of load balance. In Section 3, we propose several techniques to minimize both hiccup probability and startup latency with random, namely, N buffering with bulk request scheduling and data replication. Our simulation results demonstrate that our proposed techniques minimize hiccup probability to less than one in a million and startup latency to less than a few hundreds of milliseconds even in the worst scenario. Our conclusion and future research directions are contained in Section 4.

Display Order

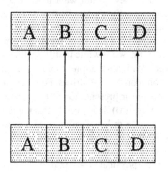

Storage Order

(a) Linear

Display Order

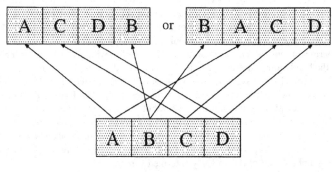

Storage Order

(b) Nonlinear (edited)

Figure 2. Continuous media presentation.

2. Data placement

We start with a discussion of the storage granularity on a single disk and compare three approaches, frame-based, block-based, and a hybrid of these two techniques. Next, Section 2.2 discusses data placement within a multi-zone disk. We describe a placement strategy that is insensitive to the frequency of access to blocks and argue why this strategy is superior. Finally, Section 2.3 analyzes the placement of data across multiple disks.

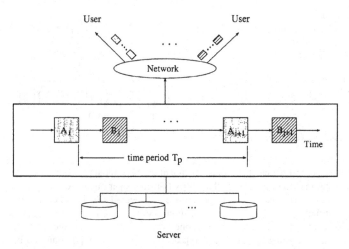

Figure 3. A hiccup free display.

2.1. Granularity of storage and retrieval

A simple and naive approach might store and retrieve data at the granularity of a frame (*FF*). Data in a frame is contiguously stored in a disk drive. This approach suffers from the following limitation. If the size of a frame is too small, the portion of wasteful work attributed to disk arm movements, i.e., seeks, becomes significant, resulting in a poor utilization of disk bandwidth [1, 9].

An alternative is to store and retrieve data at the granularity of a block, termed *BB*. A block consists of a number of frames and data in a block is contiguously stored on a disk platter. This approach is flexible because one can determine the size of a block and the number of frames it contains. For example, if the size of a block is small enough to accommodate only a single frame then it becomes identical to *FF*. With linear presentations such as movies, increasing block size maximizes the utilization of disk bandwidth. However, with nonlinear editing systems, large block sizes introduce a new limitation that wastes disk bandwidth. An edited clip produced by an editor is a sequence of shots where a shot is a sequence of frames. This sequence may consist of either one or multiple frames. Different shots might have been obtained from different parts of original clips. A transition from one shot to another may waste disk bandwidth because it might result in retrieval of irrelevant data. To elaborate, consider an editor who wants to display an edited clip that consists of 3 shots. These shots consist of 30 frames. Conceptually, if 10 frames fit per block then the system should retrieve 3 blocks, termed logical blocks. However, depending on the organization of frames across physical blocks, the number of blocks retrieved may exceed 3. For example, in figure 4, the system retrieves 5 physical blocks. The portion of data which is retrieved and not displayed constitutes wasteful work performed by the disk subsystem.

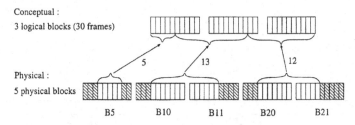

Conceptual :
3 logical blocks (30 frames)

5   13   12

Physical :
5 physical blocks

B5   B10   B11   B20   B21

Figure 4.   Disk bandwidth waste in *BB* ($N_T = 2$).

The number of transitions in a clip is dependent on its target applications. For example, while some commercials incur more than thirty transitions per minute, documentaries typically incur fewer than five transitions per minute. The degradation in system performance can be quantified as a function of the transitions. Assuming only one transition[3] occurs within a logical block, a transition invokes one extra seek (T_S: the average seek time) and block read on the average. (Appendix B relaxes this simple assumption and outlines accurate calculation based on the exact statistics of a clip.) Let T_F denote the time to read a frame and F_B to denote the number of frames in a block, then the total time (T_T) to read F_T frames with N_T transitions is:

$$T_T = \left(\left\lceil \frac{F_T}{F_B} \right\rceil + N_T \right)(T_S + F_B T_F) \tag{1}$$

In this equation, $\lceil \frac{F_T}{F_B} \rceil$ is the number of logical blocks (three in figure 4). This plus N_T (two in figure 4) defines the number of physical blocks.

One may employ a hybrid approach using both *BB* and *FF* (termed *BF*). The system can use a block-based retrieval when all the frames in a physical block are required, while applying a frame-based retrieval when only a few frames in a physical block are required. *BF* eliminates both the overhead caused by the excessive seeks with *FF* and retrieval of unnecessary data with *BB*. However, additional seeks attributed to transitions are still unavoidable. Hence, Eq. (1) can be modified as follows.

$$T_T = \left\lceil \frac{F_T}{F_B} \right\rceil (T_S + F_B T_F) + N_T T_S \tag{2}$$

Figure 5 shows the time to retrieve a one minute video clip with both the block-based (*BB*) and hybrid (*BF*) approaches. The x-axis of this figure denotes the size of a block with *BB*, measured in terms of the number of frames that fit in a block. The y-axis denotes the time to retrieve a one minute video clip. Figure 5(a) presents results for a clip that incurs 5 transitions on the average while figure 5(b) is a clip that incurs 30 transitions. Note that *FF* is a special case of *BB* or *BF* when the number of frames in a block is one. *FF* requires a longer service time when compared with both *BB* and *BF* because of the excessive seeks. With a small number of transitions ($N_T = 5$), the difference between *BB* and *BF* is insignificant.

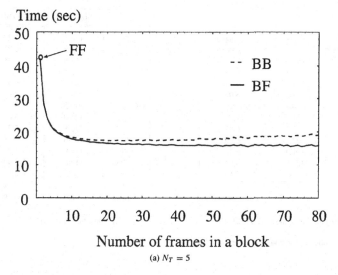

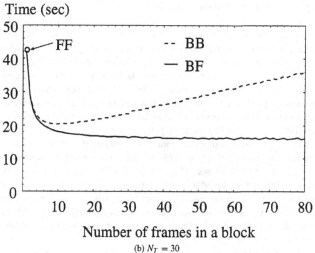

Figure 5.   Retrieval time of a one minute clip with various block sizes ($F_T = 1800$).

However, with $N_T = 30$, while the performance of *BF* remains steady as a function of block size, the performance of *BB* starts to degrade beyond a certain point. This is because each transition incurs a higher disk transfer time. In sum, *BF* is a superior alternative to both *FF* and *BB*.

Zone #	Size (MB)	Rate (MB/s)
0	506.7	8.79
1	518.3	8.74
2	164.1	8.37
3	134.5	8.03
4	116.4	7.70
5	121.1	7.41
6	119.8	6.99
7	103.2	6.66
8	101.3	6.34
9	92.0	5.94
10	84.6	5.61

Zone #	Size (MB)	Rate (MB/s)
0	136.1	7.27
1	168.9	7.07
2	155.0	6.91
3	185.5	6.76
4	105.7	6.62
5	135.9	6.45
6	140.5	6.26
7	128.0	6.09
8	275.8	5.74
9	107.6	5.48
10	114.9	5.26
11	112.6	4.99
12	107.8	4.77
13	76.4	4.54
14	100.0	4.29

(a) Seagate Barracuda 4LP, ST32171W   (b) Quantum Atlas XP32150

Figure 6. Zone information of two commercial disks.

2.2. Data placement within a multi-zone disk

Modern disk drives are produced with multiple zones to meet the demands for a higher storage capacity [18]. A zone is a contiguous collection of disk cylinders whose tracks have the same storage capacity. The outer zones provide a higher transfer rate as compared to the inner ones. This is because tracks are longer towards the outer cylinders of a disk and can store more data as compared to the inner ones. While zoning increases the storage capacity of a disk, it produces a disk that has multiple data transfer rates depending on the location of data within a disk (see figure 6 for two different disk models). Therefore, the block reading time varies significantly depending on block placement within a disk drive. For example, if a 1MB block is assigned to the outermost zone of the Seagate Barracuda disk (figure 6(a)), its transfer time is 113.8 msec. If the same block is now assigned to the innermost zone, its transfer time increases to 178.3 msec. Thus, when a server is required to support multiple media types with different bandwidth requirements (i.e., different block sizes), the block reading time will vary widely depending on the block size and its assigned zone. This may result in a higher block retrieval time and consequently a higher hiccup probability. In this section, we describe several data placement techniques and quantify their performance tradeoffs using a simulation study.

Define m as the number of zones in a disk, R_i as the data transfer rate at zone i, n as the number of media types, D_i as the bandwidth requirement of media type i ($1 \leq i \leq n$), and $B_i = T_p \times D_i$ as the block size of an object with media type i assuming a fixed time period (T_p) for all the media types. Because of multiple block sizes and disk transfer rates, the time to read a block (service time) varies depending on the location of a data block within a disk. When the system retrieves a block of type i located in zone j, its transfer time (service time)[4] is $s_{i,j} = \frac{B_i}{R_j}$. When there are b blocks in the system, the average service time is:

$$\bar{s} = \sum_{i=1}^{b} F_i \sum_{j=1}^{n} P_{i,B_j} \sum_{k=1}^{m} \frac{P_{i,Z_k} B_j}{R_k} \qquad (3)$$

where F_i is the access frequency of block i, P_{i,B_j} is the probability that the size of block i is B_j, and P_{i,Z_k} is the probability that this block is assigned to zone k. The variance of service time is:

$$\sigma_s^2 = \sum_{i=1}^{b} F_i \sum_{j=1}^{n} \sum_{k=1}^{m} P_{i,B_j} P_{i,Z_k} (s_{j,k} - \bar{s})^2 \qquad (4)$$

The block retrieval time (ω) in a multi-user environment consists of the service time and waiting time in a disk queue. It is determined by the service time and its variance when the system load and access frequency are fixed. We compare three block placement approaches in this paper.

- Random placement (RP): This simple technique assigns blocks to the zones in a random manner.
- Maximizing throughput placement (MTP): Several studies attempted to minimize the average disk service time ($\bar{s}$) by assigning large blocks with a high frequency of access to faster zones [7, 20]. MTP sorts blocks based on their size and frequency of access ($F_i \times B_i$ for each block i). Next, blocks are assigned to the zones sequentially starting with the fastest zone. Block i with the highest $F_i \times B_i$ value is assigned to the fastest zone.
- Minimizing variance placement (MVP): The objective of this technique is to reduce both the service time and its variance. With MVP, a block of size B_i is placed on the zone Z_j (with R_j) which has the closest B_i/R_j value to the average block reading time ($\bar{T}_B$):

$$\bar{T}_B = \frac{average\ block\ size}{average\ transfer\ rate} = \frac{\frac{1}{n}\sum_{i=1}^{n} B_i}{\frac{1}{m}\sum_{i=1}^{m} R_i}$$

Note that MVP is independent of frequency of access to the blocks.

We have compared these techniques using a simulation model, see Appendix A. Our performance results indicate that both MTP and MVP are superior to RP. MTP does outperform MVP at times. However, in these cases, MVP's variance in retrieval time is lower than MTP's (approximately 50% lower). One advantage of MVP is that it is not sensitive to the access frequency of objects. With MTP, if the access frequency is either inaccurate or changes over time, the placement of data could result in a low system performance. (Reorganization of data with MTP is a non-trivial research topic with a number of open-ended questions, such as When to trigger reorganization? What objects to migrate? Where to migrate these objects? etc.)

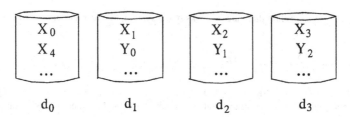

Figure 7. Round-robin placement.

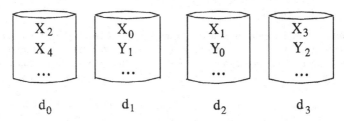

Figure 8. Random placement.

2.3. Data placement across disk drives

Assuming a system with d homogeneous disks, the data is striped [1, 8, 16] across the disks in order to distribute the load of a display evenly across the disks. There are a number of ways to assign blocks of an object to the d disks. We consider two, namely, *round-robin* and *random*. With round-robin, blocks are assigned to disks in a round-robin manner starting with an arbitrarily chosen disk [1, 11, 16]. For example, figure 7 depicts a system with four disk drives where the assignment of X starts with disk d_0. Another way to distribute the system load across the disks is to employ a random placement of data [14, 21], see figure 8.

Figure 9(a) shows the average startup latency of these two alternatives as a function of system load (utilization). Results from various configurations showed similar trends (see details in [10]). In all cases, the average startup latency with round-robin is higher than with random. With a high system utilization this difference becomes more profound. In sum, random is more appropriate for latency-sensitive applications than round-robin. Round-robin cannot support any arbitrary display order in editing application because the pattern of access to the data might change arbitrarily when an editor changes shot sequence. However, random incurs hiccups that are attributed to the statistical variation of the number of block requests per disk drive. In particular, a single disk could become a potential bottleneck with an uneven distribution of block references. Figure 9(b) shows an example of the probability of hiccups with random as a function of the system utilization. With a utilization higher than 0.8, many displays may suffer due to a high probability of hiccup. This probability must be minimized in order for random to be suitable for editing applications.

Startup Latency (sec)

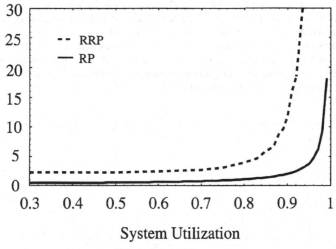

(a) Average startup latency

Prob. of Hiccup

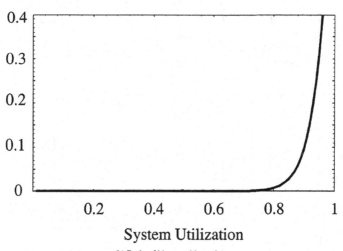

(b) Prob. of hiccup with random

Figure 9.   Round-robin vs. random.

With random, when a disk receives more than its fair share of block requests at an instance in time, it become a bottleneck for the entire system, increasing block retrieval time (ω) which consists of service time (block reading time) and waiting time in a disk queue. In this section, we measure block retrieval time with a traditional double buffering technique and describe the relation between block retrieval time and hiccup probability.

Traditionally, double buffering (figure 10(a)) has been widely used to absorb the variance of block retrieval time [8, 23, 24]. The idea is as follows: while a buffer is being consumed from memory, the system fills up another memory frame with data. The system can initiate display after the first buffer is filled and a request for the next one is issued.

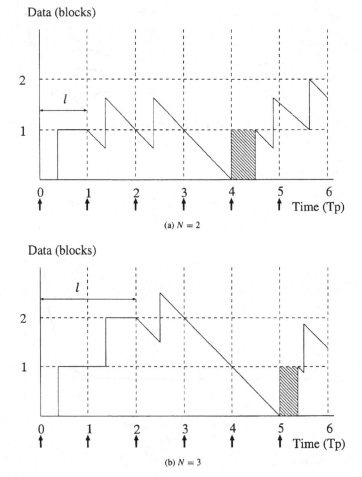

Figure 10. N buffering technique: prefetching with sequential.

Probability [ω < t]

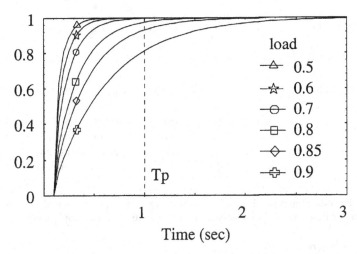

Time (sec)

Figure 11. Retrieval time distribution.

Figure 11 presents some simulation results of block retrieval time distributions with a random placement. In these simulations, we assumed that: 1) a block consisted of 30 frames and the duration of a time period was one second long ($T_p = 1$), 2) requests followed the Poisson arrival pattern, and 3) a constant service time of 100 msec based on a simple single zone disk model with a fixed disk transfer rate and a constant-bit-rate media type. Assuming a constant service time, we quantify the impact of waiting time variance attributed to random placement across disks on the distribution of retrieval time.[5] As shown in Table 1, some block requests experience retrieval times (ω) longer than the average. For example, when the system load is 0.8, 1.9% of requests experience hiccups, i.e., longer retrieval time than a time period (1.0 sec), with 0.045% of these requests experiencing delays longer than two time period (2.0 sec). With double buffering, a display does not incur a hiccup when retrieval time of a block is either equal to or less than a time period long.

In Section 3, we outline several strategies to resolve bottlenecks in order to minimize the hiccup probability with random. These techniques are N buffering with bulk request scheduling and replication. Both minimize hiccup probability and startup latency. N buffering accomplishes this by requiring a client to allocate a portion of its memory for continuous display, while data replication requires extra disk space at the server.

3. N buffering and data replication

Without loss of generality and in order to simplify the discussion, this section assumes that a logical block is equivalent to a physical block. This is because Section 2 has already

Table 1. Examples of retrieval time distributions.

Load (ρ)	$\bar{\omega}$ (msec)	Max. ω (msec)	Probability		
			$\omega > 1T_p$	$\omega > 2T_p$	$\omega > 3T_p$
0.50	151.2	1138	0.000030	0.0	0.0
0.55	162.5	1229	0.000070	0.0	0.0
0.60	176.7	1304	0.000160	0.0	0.0
0.65	195.5	1367	0.000460	0.0	0.0
0.70	220.6	1441	0.001570	0.0	0.0
0.75	256.1	2036	0.006430	0.000020	0.0
0.80	308.3	2621	0.018990	0.000450	0.0
0.85	397.9	3415	0.055720	0.002630	0.000200
0.90	597.6	4286	0.177530	0.023490	0.003140

considered the impact of a logical block translating to multiple physical blocks. We start with a description of N buffering. Next, Section 3.2 introduces data replication.

3.1. N buffering

One can generalize double buffering to N *buffering* by using N buffers and prefetching $N - 1$ blocks before initiating a display. The system can continue to request a block every time a memory buffer becomes empty. This minimizes the probability of hiccup to $p[\omega > (N - 1)T_p]$ because the retrieval time of a block must now exceed $(N - 1)$ time periods in order for a display to incur a hiccup. As demonstrated by Table 1, when the system load is 0.85, the hiccup probability decreases by a factor of 20 when N is increased from 2 to 3. With N buffering, there exist alternative ways of prefetching data and scheduling block retrievals. Figure 12 outlines a taxonomy of different techniques using a deadline

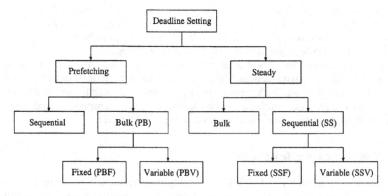

Figure 12. A taxonomy of deadline setting techniques.

driven servicing policy where each block is tagged with a deadline and the disk services requests using an earliest-deadline-first (EDF) policy.

This taxonomy differentiates between two stages of block retrieval on behalf of a display: (1) *prefetching* stage that requests the first $N - 1$ blocks and (2) *steady* stage that requests the remaining blocks. The system may employ a different policy to tag blocks that constitute each stage. Furthermore, blocks can be issued either in a *Bulk* or *Sequential* manner. With Bulk, all requests are issued at the same time while, with Sequential, requests are issued one at a time whenever a buffer in client's memory becomes free. Note that Bulk is irrelevant during a steady stage because it is very expensive to prefetch the entire clip at the client. This explains why the Bulk branch is as a leaf node of steady. Similarly, Sequential is irrelevant during prefetching because N buffers are available and our objective is to minimize startup latency.[6] The remaining leaves of the taxonomy are categorized based on how they assign deadline to each block: either *Fixed* or *Variable*. With Fixed, all block requests have identical deadlines while, with Variable, requests might have different deadlines.

During the steady stage (SS), a client issues a block request when a buffer in its memory becomes free. Typically, a memory buffer becomes free every time period because the display time of a block is one time period long. With SSF, a fixed deadline,[7] $(N - 1)T_p$, is assigned to all steady requests to maximize the tolerable variance of block retrieval time to prevent hiccups. However, with SSV, deadlines are determined by the number of blocks in the buffer. If the number of un-displayed blocks in the buffer is k when a block request is issued, then its deadline is set to $k \times T_p$. SSV strives to maintain the maximum data in the buffer by making the buffer full as soon as possible, while SSF strives to prevent the data starvation in the buffer. The results demonstrate that both techniques provide an almost identical performance.

3.1.1. PB: Bulk dispatching of blocks during prefetching stage.

With Bulk, when a clip A is referenced, $N - 1$ requests are concurrently dispatched to the server for its first $N - 1$ blocks, see figure 13(a). This section describes alternative strategies for (a) when to initiate the display of A relative to the arrival of the $N - 1$ blocks? and (b) how to set the deadline for these bulk requests? Consider each in turn. A client may initiate display in two alternative ways: either 1) once all $N - 1$ blocks have arrived, termed Conservative Display (CD), or 2) upon the arrival of block A_0, termed Aggressive Display (AD). In Section 3.1.3, we compare these two alternatives. The results demonstrate that AD is superior to CD.

The deadline assigned to the first $N - 1$ blocks can be either fixed (termed *Fixed*, PBF) or variable (termed *Variable*, PBV). With PBV, block B_i is tagged with $(i + 1)T_p$ as its deadline. Assuming that a client initiates display when all $N - 1$ blocks have arrived (i.e., CD), the startup latency is determined by the longest retrieval time of the first $N - 1$ requests, $max(\omega_0, \ldots, \omega_{N-2})$ where ω_i is the retrieval time of block B_i. PBF is more aggressive because it can set the deadline for all $N - 1$ requests to T_p in order to minimize startup latency. These requests might compete with block requests issued by other clients that are in their steady stage, increasing the probability of hiccups. However, this increase is negligible because the number of clients that are in their prefetching stage is typically small.

Section 3.1.3 compares these four alternatives, namely, PBF-CD, PBF-AD, PBV-CD, PBV-AD. The results demonstrate that PBV-AD provides a performance almost identical to PBF-AD. These two techniques are superior to the other alternatives.

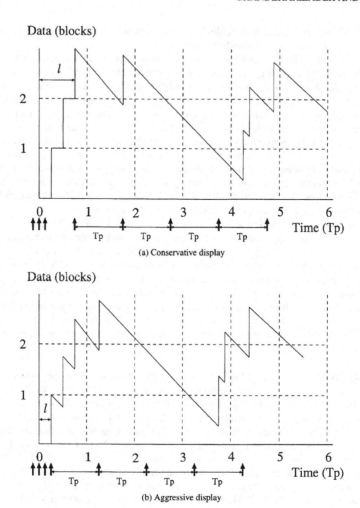

Figure 13. *N* buffering with prefetching bulk requests ($N = 4$).

3.1.2. Two approaches to handle hiccups.   While our proposed techniques strive to minimize hiccups, they cannot eliminate them all together. Moreover, the policy used at the
client to respond to a hiccup impacts the server. To elaborate, a client may respond in two
alternative ways to a hiccup: either wait for the missing data indefinitely (termed *Wait*) or
skip the missing data and continue the display with remaining blocks (termed *Skip*). In the
first case, the display is resumed upon the arrival of the missing data. This means that the
server must service all block requests, even those whose deadline has been violated. With

Skip, the server may discard these block requests because a client no longer needs them, minimizing the server load.

With Skip, in addition to skipping content with hiccups, every time that a display incurs a hiccup, the probability of it incurring another hiccup increases exponentially. This is because the waiting tolerance of N buffering decreases to that of $N - 1$ buffering since the number of buffers in the client's memory is reduced to $N - 2$. One may extend Skip to delay the display of remaining blocks by one T_p in order to prevent this undesirable situation. (There is no advantage to making Skip delay for multiple time periods.)

As detailed in Section 3.1.3, Skip results in a lower hiccup probability when compared with Wait because it reduces the server load. In passing, it is important to note that a client should not issue block requests while waiting because its buffers may overflow.

3.1.3. Evaluation.   We evaluated various techniques described in Section 3.1 using a trace driven simulation study. This trace was generated synthetically using a Poisson arrival pattern. In all simulations presented in this section, we assumed a single media type with 4Mb/s bandwidth requirement and a block size of 0.5 Mbytes ($T_p = 1$ second). Blocks were distributed across twenty Quantum Atlas XP32150 disks using random. The disk model for Quantum Atlas XP32150 disk is identical to the multi-zone model shown in figure 6(b). Our repository consisted of 50 different edited clips each consisting of 120 logical blocks. We assumed a uniform distribution of access to the clips.

All results demonstrate that the hiccup probability decreases as a function of N (number of buffers). For example, we can reduce the hiccup probability to less than one in a million by increasing the number of buffers to seven. This would be satisfactory for almost all applications.

Table 2 shows that Skip provides a lower hiccup probability than Wait because Skip minimizes server's load by not servicing requests that have already violated their deadlines. This difference becomes more profound when the number of buffers decreases because this increases the percentage of requests that miss their deadline. It is important to note that the use of Skip is application dependent. Those applications that can tolerate skipping content should use Skip in order to minimize the probability of hiccup. For the rest of this evaluation, we assume the Wait scheme.

Table 3 shows a comparison of alternative PB techniques. The results demonstrate that the probability of hiccups is almost identical with all techniques. Figure 14(a) shows the

Table 2.   Skip vs. wait (utilization $= 0.8$).

		Number of buffers (N)					
	Techniques	2	3	4	5	6	7
Avg. retrieval	Skip	296.4	338.7	348.8	351.9	352.6	352.6
time (msec)	Wait	336.6	347.9	351.9	352.4	352.6	352.6
Hiccup	Skip	0.011388	0.001195	0.000238	0.000043	0.000002	$<10^{-6}$
probability	Wait	0.042648	0.005485	0.001064	0.000212	0.000005	$<10^{-6}$

Table 3. PB techniques (utilization = 0.8).

		Number of buffers (N)					
	Techniques	2	3	4	5	6	7
Average retrieval time (msec)	PBF-CD	335.7	348.1	352.5	354.3	355.4	357.1
	PBF-AD	335.7	348.1	352.7	354.3	355.6	357.0
	PBV-CD	335.7	347.8	350.5	352.7	353.8	355.9
	PBV-AD	335.7	347.7	352.5	354.0	355.6	357.3
Hiccup probability	PBF-CD	0.041364	0.005574	0.001200	0.000293	0.000027	$<10^{-6}$
	PBF-AD	0.041364	0.005598	0.001213	0.000281	0.000023	$<10^{-6}$
	PBV-CD	0.041364	0.005276	0.001115	0.000196	0.000021	$<10^{-6}$
	PBV-AD	0.041364	0.005681	0.001212	0.000261	0.000021	$<10^{-6}$
Average startup latency (msec)	PBF-CD	318.2	186.6	148.7	195.9	206.2	224.2
	PBF-AD	318.2	148.5	140.5	139.4	138.5	139.8
	PBV-CD	318.2	369.0	375.3	380.1	389.8	420.6
	PBV-AD	318.3	147.7	139.5	138.1	136.9	137.7
Standard deviation of startup latency	PBF-CD	281.7	144.2	93.5	59.5	48.3	52.9
	PBF-AD	281.7	106.0	65.4	48.0	40.7	40.5
	PBV-CD	281.7	325.3	334.6	326.2	327.5	351.2
	PBV-AD	281.7	103.8	64.4	45.1	38.1	37.4
Worst startup latency (msec)	PBF-CD	2861	2708	2430	1883	881	512
	PBF-AD	2861	2534	2524	1999	980	406
	PBV-CD	2861	3515	4409	4373	4740	5087
	PBV-AD	2861	2552	2437	1828	891	336

average startup latency as a function of N. Figure 14(b) shows the distribution of startup latency when $N = 7$. The y-axis of this figure is the probability of a display incurring a certain startup latency. For example, the peak point of PBV-AD illustrates that 44% of displays experiences startup latency between 100 msec and 150 msec. Aggressive display (AD) approach provides a better startup latency distribution, i.e., a smaller average and variance, than the conservative display (CD) approach. Overall, both PBV-AD and PBF-AD are superior to the other alternatives when it comes to startup latency. Hence, this can satisfy almost all the latency-sensitive applications, even in the worst case scenario (336 msec), with a hiccup probability that is less than one in a million ($<10^{-6}$).

Similar trends were observed with our other simulation studies that utilized different values for parameters such as utilization, block size, number of disks. Generally, a lower hiccup probability is observed when the system utilization is lower. The number of disks does not impact the observed trends unless it is too small (less than 6). With a smaller block size, the portion of disk seek time becomes greater and it results in a higher disk utilization and a lower hiccup probability.

Avg. startup latency (msec)

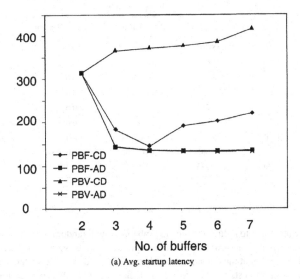

(a) Avg. startup latency

Probability

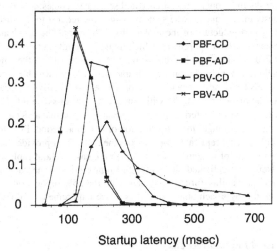

(b) Startup latency distribution ($N = 7$)

Figure 14.   Startup latency of PB techniques.

Table 4. Hiccup probability with data replication.

Load	Hiccup probability		
	No replication	25% replication	Full replication
0.50	0.000002	0.0	0.0
0.55	0.000026	0.0	0.0
0.60	0.000100	0.000001	0.0
0.65	0.000441	0.000005	0.0
0.70	0.001762	0.000018	0.0
0.75	0.006069	0.000058	0.0
0.80	0.020525	0.000231	0.0
0.85	0.067085	0.001008	0.000001
0.90	0.197485	0.023567	0.013934

3.2. Data replication

An alternative approach to reduce the hiccup probability with random is to replicate blocks. Assuming that each block has two copies, termed primary and secondary, they are randomly assigned to disks such that the two copies reside on different disks. The system can employ the disk with fewer requests when servicing a block request. To illustrate, assume that all blocks of a clip X have a secondary copy. When a request for block X_i arrives, the system locates the two disks that contain its primary and secondary copies. After comparing the number of requests in two queues, the system assigns the request to the disk with fewer requests, resulting in a reduction of the probability of hiccups. The disadvantage of data replication is its extra space requirement, which might be significant due to the large clip sizes. We quantified the hiccup probability with random while varying the amount of extra space for replication. In our simulations, we assumed fifty movies which are one-hour long and requires a 4Mb/s bandwidth. The total database size was 90 GBytes in size.

Table 4 shows the hiccup probability with various amount of space for replication. We assumed a traditional double buffering in these simulations such that a hiccup occurs when the block retrieval time is longer than the duration of one time period. First, we randomly selected 25% of blocks and replicated them across the disks. This provides a hiccup probability that is two orders of magnitude smaller than the case without replication (see the third column). Next, we replicated all blocks (full replication) in the database. This minimizes the hiccup probability further compared with the 25% replication, see the fourth column. However, this approach doubles the disk space requirement (180 GBytes of total disk space).

4. Conclusion and future directions

This paper describes the requirements and design of client-server architectures in support of nonlinear editing systems. Due to lack of space, we focused on the server side of the system. After analyzing the tradeoffs between frame and block based retrieval, we proposed a hybrid approach to maximize the bandwidth utilization. We also compared two alternative data placement strategies for a multi-disk platform and showed that a random placement incurs a lower startup latency compared with a round-robin placement. Subsequently, we proposed and evaluated buffering techniques to minimize both the hiccup probability and startup latency with random placement. We are extending our approach for the synchronized presentation of multimedia such as a video and eight audio channels. We are also investigating several possible client-server models for nonlinear editing systems that include local disk caching for continuous media data.

Appendix A: Evaluation of data placement techniques with a multi-zone disk

Based on simulations, we quantified the average block retrieval time with multiple cases of access frequencies and different block placement approaches. In our simulations, we used two different disk models (their zone information is listed in figure 6 and three media types ($M_1 = 10$Mb/s, $M_2 = 7.5$Mb/s, and $M_3 = 5$Mb/s) with three block sizes ($B_1 = 1.25$ MBytes, $B_2 = 0.94$ MBytes, and $B_3 = 0.63$ MBytes) assuming a fixed time period ($T_p = 1$ sec). We assumed that each media type consists of the same number of objects and varied the frequency of access to the objects as follows:

- Case 1: $M_1 = 0.33$, $M_2 = 0.33$, $M_3 = 0.33$: all objects have the same access frequency
- Case 2: $M_1 = 0.2$, $M_2 = 0.3$, $M_3 = 0.5$: objects with higher bandwidth requirements have lower access frequencies
- Case 3: $M_1 = 0.5$, $M_2 = 0.3$, $M_3 = 0.2$: objects with higher bandwidth requirements have higher access frequencies

We used an open simulation model for this study. The arrival rate of block requests follows the Poisson distribution. For each case, we quantified the average service time ($\bar{s}$) and the average retrieval time ($\bar{\omega}$) for the three alternative placement techniques.

Tables 5 and 6 show the simulation results with different case studies and demonstrate the impact of data placement on the average service time, the variance of service time, and the average retrieval time while varying the arrival rate of block requests.[8] In all simulations, MTP minimizes the average service time while MVP minimizes the variance in service time. With Cases 1 and 3, MVP and MTP are almost identical in placing data blocks. Consequently, their results are almost identical and superior to RP. With Case 2, MTP and RP produces better average retrieval time than MVP when the arrival rate is low. However, while we increase the arrival rate, the average retrieval times of MTP and RP increase faster than that of MVP and finally MVP produces the best result when the arrival rate is high (figure 15). This is because the variance of the service time becomes more important in determining the average retrieval time when the system load becomes higher. Moreover, even though MVP has a longer average retrieval time than both MTP and RP with a low system load (less than 10% longer), the distribution of the retrieval time is more desirable than both of MTP and RP (two examples in Tables 7 and 8) minimizing hiccup probability (see Section 3). MVP is superior to both MTP and RP in all cases when the arrival rate is high.

Table 5. Comparison (Quantum Atlas XP32150 disk).

	Placement	$\bar{s}$ (msec)	σ_s	$\bar{\omega}$ (msec)					
				$\lambda = 3.5$	$\lambda = 4.0$	$\lambda = 4.5$	$\lambda = 5.0$	$\lambda = 5.5$	$\lambda = 6.0$
Case 1	RP	154.8	53.9	264.5	314.8	412.7	706.1	–	–
	MVP	153.6	23.2	246.7	281.1	334.8	432.2	657.3	–
	MTP	153.7	23.1	247.0	281.4	335.4	433.2	659.5	–
Case 2	RP	137.9	49.5	214.3	240.7	281.3	355.2	543.1	–
	MVP	145.9	21.7	224.6	251.7	290.6	353.7	472.5	771.3
	MTP	132.1	58.3	204.2	228.8	266.4	336.3	531.5	–
Case 3	RP	172.3	54.8	332.0	432.7	731.4	–	–	–
	MVP	161.7	22.9	271.6	317.1	395.3	563.3	–	–
	MTP	161.8	22.8	271.8	317.4	395.8	564.3	–	–

Table 6. Comparison (Seagate Barracuda 4LP, ST32171W disk).

	Placement	$\bar{s}$ (msec)	σ_s	$\bar{\omega}$ (msec)					
				$\lambda = 5.5$	$\lambda = 6.0$	$\lambda = 6.5$	$\lambda = 7.0$	$\lambda = 7.5$	$\lambda = 8.0$
Case 1	RP	117.3	45.1	272.2	366.7	794.1	–	–	–
	MVP	115.9	20.1	223.1	257.4	311.7	410.4	631.0	–
	MTP	116.0	20.0	223.2	257.6	312.0	410.9	632.0	–
Case 2	RP	102.5	40.9	187.3	213.3	255.7	338.2	979.7	–
	MVP	109.5	18.3	195.5	218.6	251.7	303.3	394.2	585.9
	MTP	101.0	41.1	181.0	203.8	238.5	301.5	500.1	–
Case 3	RP	132.9	46.1	476.1	–	–	–	–	–
	MVP	123.2	20.2	262.5	319.7	432.4	758.9	–	–
	MTP	123.2	20.2	262.6	319.9	432.7	759.3	–	–

One drawback of MTP is that it requires accurate access frequency of blocks. It is not always possible to estimate the access frequency of a block at the time of data block placing. Moreover, the access frequency of blocks may evolve over time. In such an environment, MTP can be the worst choice of block placement when access frequency of blocks changes. For example, suppose that access frequency changes to Case 1 after blocks are assigned to the zones based on the access frequency of Case 2. Then MTP produces the average retrieval time of 330.6 msec ($\lambda = 4.0$) with Quantum disk which is longer than that of both MVP and RP (see Case 1 in Table 5). Changing access frequency from Case 2 to Case 3 produces the same trend.

Time (msec)

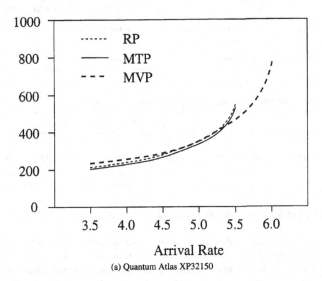

(a) Quantum Atlas XP32150

Time (msec)

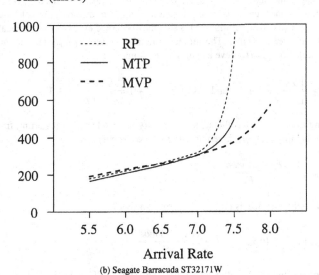

(b) Seagate Barracuda ST32171W

Figure 15. Retrieval time with Case 2.

119

Table 7. Retrieval time distribution with Case 2 ($\lambda = 4.5$) (Quantum disk).

Placement	$\bar{s}$	σ_s	$\bar{\omega}$	$P[\omega > T_p]$	$P[\omega > 2T_p]$	$P[\omega > 3T_p]$	$P[\omega > 4T_p]$
RP	137.9	49.5	281.3	0.0187	0.00057	0	0
MVP	145.9	21.7	290.6	0.0095	0	0	0
MTP	132.1	58.3	266.4	0.0186	0.00081	0	0

Table 8. Retrieval time distribution with Case 2 ($\lambda = 5.0$) (Quantum disk).

Placement	$\bar{s}$	σ_s	$\bar{\omega}$	$P[\omega > T_p]$	$P[\omega > 2T_p]$	$P[\omega > 3T_p]$	$P[\omega > 4T_p]$
RP	137.9	49.5	355.2	0.0516	0.00858	0.00191	0.000096
MVP	145.9	21.7	353.7	0.0329	0.00129	0.000055	0
MTP	132.1	58.3	336.3	0.0499	0.0088	0.0033	0.00071

Appendix B: Expected time to retrieve a clip

An edited clip is a sequence of shots; a shot is one or multiple frames generated and recorded contiguously and represents a continuous action in time and space. A shot is a sequence of frames; a frame is an image and the smallest meaningful entity in video. We can quantify the time to retrieve a shot with BF approach. Let F_S denote the number of frames in a shot and F_B to denote the number of frames in a block. The number of seeks to retrieve a shot, F_S contiguous frames, depends on the location of those frames on physical blocks. For example, when F_S is 15 and F_B is 10, this shot may be stored either in two physical blocks (2 seeks) or in three (3 seeks). The minimum number of seeks (S_{min}) and the maximum number of seeks (S_{max}) to retrieve a shot with F_S frames is:

$$S_{min} = \left\lfloor \frac{F_S - 1}{F_B} \right\rfloor + 1 \quad \text{and} \quad S_{max} = S_{min} + 1 = \left\lceil \frac{F_S - 1}{F_B} \right\rceil + 1$$

Assuming every frame has the same probability to be selected as a starting frame in a shot, the probability that S_{max} is required to retrieve a shot is:

$$P[S_{max}] = \frac{(F_S - 1) \bmod F_B}{F_B}$$

The probability that S_{min} is required to retrieve a shot is:

$$P[S_{min}] = 1 - P[S_{max}] = 1 - \frac{(F_S - 1) \bmod F_B}{F_B}$$

Thus, the expected number of seeks in retrieving a shot is: $P[S_{max}] \times S_{max} + P[S_{min}] \times S_{min}$. When an edited clip contains N_T transitions, i.e., $N_T + 1$ shots with F_{S_i} ($i = 0, \ldots, N_T$), and the total number of frame $F_T = \sum_{i=0}^{N_T} F_{S_i}$, the total number of seeks to retrieve this clip is:

$$E[S] = \sum_{i=0}^{N_T} \left[\frac{(F_{S_i} - 1) \bmod F_B}{F_B} \left(\left\lceil \frac{F_{S_i} - 1}{F_B} \right\rceil + 1 \right) \right.$$

$$\left. + \left(1 - \frac{(F_{S_i} - 1) \bmod F_B}{F_B} \right) \left(\left\lfloor \frac{F_{S_i} - 1}{F_B} \right\rfloor + 1 \right) \right]$$

Hence, the total time to read this clip is:

$$T_T = E[S]T_S + F_T T_F$$

where T_S is the average seek time and T_F is the time to read a frame.

Acknowledgments

This research was supported in part by a HP unrestricted cash/equipment gift, and the National Science Foundation under grants IRI-9203389, IRI-9258362 (NYI award), and ERC grant EEC-9529152.

Notes

1. The movie is subsequently edited by the director to a shorter version. Since the editors are simultaneously manipulating a copy, scenes shown in a trailer may not appear in the final cut.
2. Because air-time for showing of the trailer is purchased in advance. For broadcasters that carry with special events (e.g., SuperBowl), air-time might have been purchased several months in advance.
3. We assume that a transition is a switch from the current physical block to a different one.
4. Seek time is not considered in this calculation for a simple discussion. Seek time can be considered as a constant and added to $s_{i,j}$.
5. We exclude the impact of service time variance attributed to the data placement techniques within a multi-zone disk in Section 2.2 from this discussion.
6. If block requests are issued sequentially during the prefetching stage, the startup latency would increase as a linear function of N, see figure 10.
7. We are using this notation for simplicity in this paper but the real deadline is $t_{issue} + (N - 1)T_p$, where t_{issue} is the time that this request is issued.
8. In these tables, a '–' denotes the occurrence of hiccups: a retrieval time larger than the duration of a time period ($T_p = 1$ sec in our simulations).

References

1. S. Berson, S. Ghandeharizadeh, R. Muntz, and X. Ju, "Staggered striping in multimedia information systems," in Proceedings of the ACM SIGMOD International Conference on Management of Data, 1994, pp. 79–89.
2. S.M. Chung (Ed.), Multimedia Information Storage and Management, Kluwer Academic Publishers, 1996.
3. P.J. Denning, "The working set model for program behavior," Communications of the ACM, Vol. 11, No. 5, pp. 323–333, 1968.

4. M. Garofalakis, B. Ozden, and A. Silberschatz, "Resource scheduling in enhanced pay-per-view continuous media databases," in Proceedings of the International Conference on Very Large Databases, 1997.
5. A. Ghafoor, "Special issue on multimedia database systems," ACM Multimedia Systems, Vol. 3, Nos. 5/6, 1995.
6. S. Ghandeharizadeh, R. Hull, and D. Jacobs, "Design, implementation, and application of heraclitus [Alg,C]," ACM Transactions on Database Systems, Vol. 21, No. 3, 1996.
7. S. Ghandeharizadeh, D. Ierardi, D. Kim, and R. Zimmermann, "Placement of data in multi-zone disk drives," in Proceedings of Second International Baltic Workshop on DB and IS, June 1996.
8. S. Ghandeharizadeh and S.H. Kim, "Striping in multi-disk video servers," in High-Density Data Recording and Retrieval Technologies, Proc. SPIE 2604, October 1995, pp. 88–102.
9. S. Ghandeharizadeh, S.H. Kim, and C. Shahabi, "On configuring a single disk continuous media server," in Proceedings of the ACM SIGMETRICS, May 1995.
10. S. Ghandeharizadeh, S.H. Kim, and C. Shahabi, "On disk scheduling and data placement for continuous media," Submitted to IEEE Tansactions on Knowledge and Data Engineering.
11. S. Ghandeharizadeh, S.H. Kim, W. Shi, and R. Zimmermann, "On minimizing startup latency in scalable continuous media servers," in Proceedings of Multimedia Computing and Networking, Proc. SPIE 3020, February 1997, pp. 144–155.
12. Ng C. Hock, Queueing Modeling Fundamentals, John Wiley & Sons, 1996, p. 140.
13. L. Kleinrock, Queueing systems Volume I: Theory, Wiley-Interscience, 1975, p. 105.
14. R. Muntz, J. Santos, and S. Berson, "RIO: A real-time multimedia object server," ACM Sigmetrics Performance Evaluation Review, Vol. 25, No. 2, 1997.
15. T.A. Ohanian, Digital Nonlinear Editing—New Approaches to Editing Film and Video, Focal Press, 1993.
16. B. Ozden, R. Rastogi, and A. Silberschatz, "Disk striping in video server environments," in IEEE International Conference on Multimedia Computing and System, June 1995.
17. P. Rangan and H. Vin, "Efficient storage techniques for digital continuous media," IEEE Transactions on Knowledge and Data Engineering, Vol. 5, No. 4, 1993.
18. C. Ruemmler and J. Wilkes, "An introduction to disk drive modeling," IEEE Computer, 1994.
19. V.S. Subrahmanian and S. Jajodia (Eds.), Multimedia Database Systems, Springer, 1996.
20. R. Tewari, R. King, D. Kandlur, and D.M. Dias, "Placement of multimedia blocks on zoned disks," in Proceedings of Multimedia Computing and Networking, January 1996.
21. R. Tewari, R. Mukherjee, D.M. Dias, and H.M. Vin, "Design and performance tradeoffs in clustered video servers," in Proceedings of IEEE ICMCS, June 1995.
22. R. Tewari, R. Mukherjee, D.M. Dias, and H.M. Vin, "Design and performance tradeoffs in clustered video servers," in IEEE International Conference on Multimedia Computing and System, June 1996.
23. F.A. Tobagi, J. Pang, R. Baird, and M. Gang, "Streaming RAID—A disk array management system for video files," in Proceedings of the First ACM Conference on Multimedia, August 1993.
24. P.S. Yu, M.S. Chen, and D.D. Kandlur, "Design and analysis of a grouped sweeping scheme for multimedia storage management," in Proceedings of the Third International Workshop on Network and Operating System Support for Digital Audio and Video, November 1992.

Shahram Ghandeharizadeh received his Ph.D. degree in Computer Science from the University of Wisconsin, Madison, in 1990. Since then, he has been on the faculty at the University of Southern California. In 1992, Dr.

Ghandeharizadeh received the National Science Foundation Young Investigator's Award for his research on the physical design of parallel database systems. In 1995, he received an award from the School of Engineering at USC in recognition of his research activities. His primary research interests include design and implementation of multimedia storage managers, parallel database systems, and active databases. His activities are supported by several grants from the National Science Foundation, Department of Defense, and Hewlett-Packard.

Seon Ho Kim received his B.S. degree in Electronic Engineering from the Yonsei University, Korea, in 1986, and his M.S. degree in Electrical Engineering from the University of Southern California, Los Angeles, in 1994. He is currently a Ph.D. candidate in Computer Science Department at the University of Southern California. His research interests include multimedia information systems, continuous media servers, and nonlinear editing servers.

Super-Streaming: A New Object Delivery Paradigm for Continuous Media Servers

CYRUS SHAHABI   cshahabi@cs.usc.edu
MOHAMMAD H. ALSHAYEJI   alshayej@cs.usc.edu
*Integrated Media Systems Center and Computer Science Department, University of Southern California,
Los Angeles, California 90089, USA*

Abstract. A number of studies have focused on the design of continuous media, CM, (e.g., video and audio) servers to support the real-time delivery of CM objects. These systems have been deployed in local environments such as hotels, hospitals and cruise ships to support media-on-demand applications. They typically *stream* CM objects to the clients with the objective of minimizing the buffer space required at the client site. This objective can now be relaxed due to the availability of inexpensive storage devices at the client side. Therefore, we propose a *Super-streaming* paradigm that can utilize the client side resources in order to improve the utilization of the CM server. To support super-streaming, we propose a technique to enable the CM servers to deliver CM objects at a rate higher than their display bandwidth requirement. We also propose alternative admission control policies to downgrade super-streams in favor of regular streams when the resources are scarce. We demonstrate the superiority of our paradigm over streaming with both analytical and simulation models.

Moreover, new distributed applications such as distant-learning, digital libraries, and home entertainment require the delivery of CM objects to geographically disbursed clients. For quality purposes, recently many studies proposed dedicated distributed architectures to support these types of applications. We extend our super-streaming paradigm to be applicable in such distributed architectures. We propose a sophisticated resource management policy to support super-streaming in the presence of multiple servers, network links and clients. Due to the complexity involved in modeling these architectures, we only evaluate the performance of super-streaming by a simulation study.

Keywords: continuous media delivery, continuous media servers, video on demand, distributed systems

1. Introduction

The past decade has witnessed an immense interest in the design of techniques to support a hiccup-free display of continuous media (CM), video and audio, using disk-based servers [2, 4, 5, 10, 12, 20, 38–40, 46, 47, 51]. For collections see [3, 9, 15, 22, 25, 34, 44]. These servers are expected to play a major role in several emerging applications, e.g., digital libraries, health-care information systems, and distant-learning applications to name a few. Almost all the previous studies made the following two major design decisions:

1. They strive to fix the delivery rate of CM objects to their display bandwidth requirement,[1] R_c. This has been done in order to minimize the client side buffer requirement. In this paper, we denote this paradigm as *Streaming*.
2. They assumed a client-server model, which we term as a *2-level architecture* in this paper.

Although these decisions were necessary before to focus on the design of centralized CM servers, we now believe that the field is mature enough to challenge both of these design decisions. Our argument to challenge the former is that with current technological advancements, it is not far-fetched to assume clients with large and inexpensive disk/memory storage whether their end system is a PC, a PC/TV or a set-top box. We, hence, propose a *Super-streaming* paradigm that supports the delivery of CM objects at a rate higher than their display bandwidth requirement by utilizing the client site buffer (i.e., disk and/or memory). Note that super-streaming subsumes streaming.

The second decision, a 2-level architecture, is appropriate for clients in a local environment such as a hotel, hospital or a classroom. However, when users are geographically disbursed, a 2-level architecture results in a high communication cost. This is because a dedicated network line is required between every client and the main server. Moreover, the bandwidth requirement for this server is estimated to be as high as 1.54Pb/s (Peta-bit per second) for the continental United States [33]. Therefore, a number of studies [8, 18, 33] suggested different hierarchical and non-hierarchical architectures consisting of many CM servers connected via dedicated network lines. With these distributed architectures, there exist many intermediate nodes between a server delivering a CM object to a client requesting the object. We term these architectures collectively as an *m-level architecture*. With *m*-level architecture, each intermediate node can now have extra buffer space that can be utilized by the super-streaming paradigm. Hence, at different links along the delivery path, the CM object can be delivered at different rates.

In this paper, we start by describing our super-streaming paradigm assuming a 2-level architecture. Subsequently, we extend it to an m-level architecture. To realize the advantage of the super-streaming paradigm, consider the following simple scenario. Assume a 2-level architecture where two nodes are connected to each other via an OC-3 channel (with 155Mb/s bandwidth capacity). One node is a continuous media server and the other node is a client (e.g., a set-top box). Now assume that the client requests a 2 hour MPEG-2 movie with a display bandwidth requirement of 4Mb/s. To support this client, two delivery approaches have been discussed in the literature. First, to utilize 4Mb/s of the OC-3 channel and stream the video to the user [31]. Second, to utilize the entire 155Mb/s of the channel and dump the video to the client's disk buffer as fast as possible [13]. The first approach has the advantage of not requiring any disk buffer at the user site (as opposed to 3.6GB with the second approach). Instead, the second approach has the advantage of utilizing the entire link bandwidth and freeing it up after 2 minutes (as opposed to 2 hours with the first approach). Either of these approaches might be reasonable depending on the system load and client resources. Therefore, our proposed super-streaming paradigm is designed to not only cover these two extreme cases but also everything in between.

To support super-streaming, CM servers are required to guarantee multiple delivery rates per object. For example, a server may need to deliver an MPEG-2 video object with $R_c = 4$Mb/s at a rate of 8Mb/s, 12Mb/s or 20Mb/s. Therefore, we propose a technique to enable the CM servers to support multiple delivery rates per object. This multiple delivery rate solution is not only applicable to our paradigm but can be utilized by other applications such as news-on-demand. With news-on-demand, it is essential to make news available to users as fast as possible. Therefore, the system must be able to accept new news clips at five or even ten times their regular consumption rates. Since reading and writing CM objects can be considered as dual problems, finding a solution to one automatically solves the other. Hence, if a server can read CM objects at multiple delivery rates, then it should be able to write CM objects at multiple rates also.

The major contributions of this paper discussed for both 2-level and m-level architectures are:

1. A super-streaming paradigm that can utilize resources, that are otherwise unused, to support a display.
2. A resource management policy that attempts to improve the total resource utilization by maximizing the resources dedicated to super-streams.
3. An admission control policy that differentiates between super-streams and regular streams in order to be fair.
4. A technique that enable CM servers to support multiple delivery rates that is not only essential for our paradigm but can be utilized by other applications.
5. An analytical and a simulation model to evaluate the performance of super-streaming which demonstrates its superiority over streaming.

2. Related work

To meet the real-time requirements of CM objects, a significant amount of research was conducted on centralized multimedia servers (e.g., [21, 24, 27, 31]). These servers stream CM objects to the client to minimize the need for client side buffer. In this study, we propose a super-streaming paradigm that utilizes client side resources to improve system performance (2-level architecture). Meanwhile, other studies (e.g., [14, 26, 36, 41, 43, 49, 50]) focused on supporting CM objects on high-speed networks. Marrying these two technologies (server and network) will produce an m-level architecture that can achieve the cost effective delivery of CM objects to users. Therefore, we extended our paradigm to make it applicable to the m-level architecture.

Some studies focused on providing cost effective MOD services over the Internet [35, 45, 48]. However, due to network bandwidth limitations as well as the best effort nature of the Internet components and protocols, some Quality of Service (QoS) negotiation and adaptation are required [19, 28, 32]. Even then, the resulted service can not match the quality of display expected by (say) pay-per-view or video rental customers. Therefore, [7, 8, 18, 33, 37] proposed a dedicated hierarchical distributed server that can provide a service that matches or exceeds the quality of display available through pay-per-view and video rental. At the lowest level of the hierarchy are the head-end nodes to which users are connected. Asymmetric digital subscriber line (ADSL) seems to be the strongest candidate for connecting users to these head-end nodes [29]. The higher levels of the hierarchy, however, are typically based on the asynchronous transfer mode (ATM) technology. These systems are perfect examples of our m-level architecture. Hence, our super-streaming paradigm can be employed by these systems in a straightforward manner.

A number of admission control policies have been proposed for CM servers [6, 16, 30]. However, these studies assume a single delivery rate (constant or variable) per object. With super-streaming, objects can be delivered to clients at rates higher than their consumption rates thus significantly changing the admission control problem. In this paper, we propose an admission control policy that handles upgrading and downgrading object delivery rates in order to optimize the utilization of resources.

Other studies have considered utilizing client side buffer (memory and/or disk) in the context of client-server databases (e.g., [17]). However, the goals of these systems differ from those of CM server. While these studies focused on reducing response time, our work focuses on improving the system performance while meeting the real-time requirements of CM objects.

3. *2-Level* architecture (client-server model)

In this section, we describe our super-streaming paradigm assuming a *2-Level* architecture. First, we describe a technique to extend CM servers so that they can support super-streams, i.e., the objects that are delivered faster than their display rate. Next, we discuss two alternative resource management policies to assign extra server, network and client site resources to requests in order to support super-streaming. Finally, we propose two alternative admission control policies to deal with the extra resources occupied by active super-streams in order to accept or reject new requests in need of these resources.

Figure 1 depicts a client server VOD system. As argued in [11], the use of client side buffer (memory and/or disk) has a number of advantages such as:

1. Reducing the effect of delivery rate and consumption rate mismatch.
2. Making the server and network real-time requirements less stringent.
3. Allowing the server a more flexible delivery thus improving the server load balancing.
4. Providing a more efficient support for some VCR operations.

In this section, we discuss how the flexibility in delivery (i.e., the ability to deliver CM objects at a rate higher than their consumption rate) can be exploited to improve the system throughput.

In figure 1, the client is connected to the multimedia server via a dedicated network line such as ADSL.[2] A client submits a request to the server, and subsequently, the request is

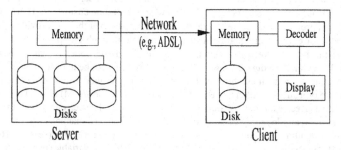

Figure 1. The client-server architecture.

either served immediately, or rejected if it requires resources that are not available. With streaming, once the request is accepted, the encoded data is delivered to the client at the rate of consumption R_c. After a temporary stage in memory, the data is decoded and then displayed.

Super-streaming, however, attempts to utilize otherwise idle resources (during off-peak periods) to expedite the delivery of CM objects hoping to make more resources available to future requests. With super-streaming, objects can be delivered at a rate higher than their display rate. Therefore, a client side buffer is required to store the data that is delivered but not yet displayed. The maximum amount of data that super-streaming can buffer at the client can be computed using Eq. (1), where R_l is the bandwidth on the link connecting the client to the server, R_c is the object display bandwidth requirement and $Object_{size}$ is the size of the object.

$$max\_buffer\_size = \frac{(R_l - R_c) * Object_{size}}{R_l} \tag{1}$$

Trivially, if the client buffer size is greater than or equal to the max_buffer_size computed by Eq. (1), the system can deliver the object to the client at R_l without the risk of data loss. However, if the client buffer size is less than max_buffer_size, special care is needed to avoid overflowing the client buffer. That is, the system can still initiate a super-stream with a delivery rate of R_l, but needs to downgrade it to a regular stream with a delivery rate of R_c once the buffer is full.

3.1. Multiple delivery rates

Typically, CM servers can support a single delivery rate R_c, per stored CM object. However, to support the super-streaming paradigm, CM servers are required to support higher delivery rates for those objects that are super-streamed to the client. In this section, we propose a technique to extend the CM servers to support super-streams.

Centralized CM servers, such as [31], are typically multi-disk systems that employ stripping techniques to improve load balancing and throughput. To store an object X, the system partitions it into f subobjects: $X_1, X_2, \ldots, X_f$ (see [23] for the computation of the size of a subobject). These subobjects are then placed on disks (each disk can itself be a cluster of disk drives) in a round-robin manner (figure 2). The time to display a subobject

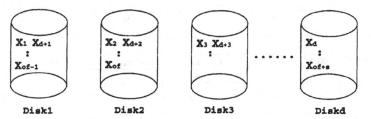

Figure 2. Round-robin assignment.

is termed a *time interval*. To support simultaneous display of several objects, a time interval is divided into slots, with each slot corresponding to the retrieval time of a subobject from a disk. Once object X is referenced, its display employs a cycle-based approach: the server sends the first subobject of X to the user during the first time interval and its display is initiated at the beginning of the second time interval. During the second time interval, the server sends X_2 to the user which initiates its display at the beginning of the third time interval. This process is repeated until all subobjects of X have been retrieved and displayed. By employing this approach, the server is able to deliver X to the user at the rate of consumption. This system is not geared toward delivering X at any other rate. However, with super-streaming, the server may need to deliver X at three or four times R_c. To achieve this, we propose a multiple delivery rate technique.

Suppose that a server needs to deliver the object X at a rate of $2R_c$. In this case, two subobjects of X need to be delivered per time interval. An immediate solution might be to send consecutive subobjects per time interval, i.e., send X_1 and X_2 in the first time interval, X_3 and X_4 in the second time interval, and so on. However, due to round-robin assignment of the subobjects to disks, this technique will result in a complicated scheduling. An alternative technique is to partition X (logically) into two equi-size portions, $(A = X_1..X_{of-1})$ and $(B = X_{of}..X_f)$ (figure 3(a)). Subsequently, to support a rate of $2R_c$, two independent streams are initiated (S_1 starting at X_1) and (S_2 starting at X_{of}). This way, the system can follow its regular scheduling technique by treating these two as independent streams. Note that since the client will consume X at the rate of R_c, the out of sequence arrival of X_{of+i}'s subobjects will be buffered for later consumption and will not interfere with sequential consumption of X_{1+j}'s subobjects.

A scheduling problem may arise when the start of the second stream X_{of} falls in a slot that is occupied by other streams. This is because the system cannot delay the delivery of the second stream until a slot becomes available. In this case, the server can compensate by increasing the length of either the first portion or the second portion. Increasing the length of the second portion is not an option since it may result in a buffer overflow at the client side. By increasing the length of the first portion, the system shifts the start of the second stream to the first available slot. To illustrate, in figure 2, the start of the second stream X_{of} falls on an occupied slot. The system compensated by shifting the start of the second

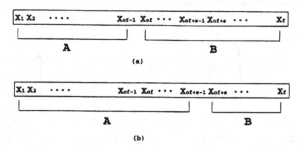

Figure 3. Object partitioning.

portion to the subsequent subobject of X that falls on the first available slot (say X_{of+s} in figure 2(b)).

This solution can be generalized to enable CM servers to support any multiple of R_c. That is, if a rate of nR_c is required, and the server has enough resources to support this rate, the object can be partitioned into n equi-size portions and n independent streams are initiated from the start of each of these portions.

As mentioned earlier, with super-streaming, if the client buffer size is not as large as *max_buffer_size* (see Eq. (1)) then nR_c cannot be supported for the entire delivery. In this case, the system starts nR_c delivery and then reduces the rate to R_c. This can be achieved by enforcing a larger first portion for the referenced object X and smaller $n - 1$ portions. The total size of the last $n - 1$ portions is hence determined by the client buffer size.

It is important to point out that the proposed solution is not only applicable to our application but can be employed by other applications such as news-on-demand. With news-on-demand, it is essential to make news available to users as fast as possible. Therefore, the system must be able to download new news clips at $5R_c$ or $10R_c$. Since reading and writing continuous media objects can be considered as dual problems, finding a solution to one automatically solves the other. To transfer an object at a rate of nR_c, n reading streams at the sender and n writing streams at the receiver can be established.

The multiple delivery rate solution we proposed is restricted to delivering the object at nR_c where n is an integer. Supporting non-integer multiple rates is a more challenging task which we plan to tackle as our future research.

3.2. Resource management

The amount of resources that can be utilized by super-streams depends on a number of factors such as: available server, link, and client bandwidths as well as the client buffer capacity. Hence, a policy is required to identify idle resources and assign them to the eligible super-streams. With our 2-level architecture, each client has its own buffer and a dedicated link connecting it to the server. Hence, the only resource under competition is the server bandwidth. Therefore, the goal of the resource management policy is to maximize the utilization of this shared resource.

One policy may examine the system resources upon the arrival of a new request and assign the maximum amount of resources to this request. The request holds on to these resources (unless downgraded)[3] until it terminates. When the request terminates the resources are released. We termed this approach *Assign and Release* (*A&R*). The main drawback of this approach is that it does not utilize any released resources due to other requests downgrades or terminations (i.e., these resources will remain idle until the arrival of a new request).

An alternative approach, termed *Assign and Reassign* (*A&RA*), not only assigns the maximum amount of resources to newly arriving requests but also attempts to reassign any resources made available by the downgrading or the departure of other active requests. To achieve this, the system labels requests capable of utilizing more resources than what they are actually holding as *upgradable*. The system then reacts to the release of resources by locating an upgradable request and assigning free resources to it. The system will continue to do so until it runs out of either free resources or upgradable requests. As mentioned earlier, the goal of resource management in the *2-Level* architecture is to maximize the utilization of the server and thus have no reason to favor one upgradable request over the others. Therefore, if more than one upgradable request exist, the system can select one at random. If the selected request is not capable of utilizing all the free resources, the system will assign the maximum amount of resources to this request and allocate the rest to another upgradable request(s). The performance of these alternative approaches is compared in Section 3.5 and the results demonstrate the superiority of *A&RA*.

3.3. Admission control

With streaming, admission control is straightforward: when a new request arrives and the system has the required resources, then the request is accepted; otherwise, it is rejected. Employing super-streaming, however, introduces new admission control alternatives that did not exist with streaming. In this section, we discuss these admission control alternatives.

With super-streaming, a newly arrived request may need resources that are utilized by some super-streams. In this case, the system may adopt one of the following approaches:

1. *Non-preemptive*: reject the new request.
2. *Preemptive*: downgrade one or more super-streams to free enough resources in order to accept the new request.

Although simple, the non-preemptive approach does not treat requests fairly. It rejects the new request, while allowing super-streams to occupy more resources than required. Therefore, employing this approach may lead to a high rejection rate.

By downgrading super-streams, the preemptive approach is attempting to achieve fair treatment of requests. However, this approach is more challenging. With this approach, the admission control policy needs to decide: 1) if downgrading one or more super-streams will free enough resources to admit the new request, and 2) which super-streams to downgrade in the presence of multiple candidates. Employing *A&RA* resource management within the *2-Level* architecture ensures that no resources remain free in the existence of an upgradable request. Therefore, the admission control policy can locate a super-stream at random and downgrades it to free enough resources to admit the new request. This will continue until the request is admitted or the system runs out of super-streams thus causing the rejection of the new request. Note that the admission control policy does not actually start downgrading super-streams until it ensures that these downgrades will lead to the admission of the new request. It is also important to point out that when a super-stream is downgraded to a regular stream, it maintains the minimum amount of resources needed to sustain the quality of display expected by the user. For the remainder of this section, preemptive admission control policy is assumed. However, the performance of the two policies will be compared within our *m-Level* architecture in Section 4.4.

3.4. Analytical model

To compare the performance of super-streaming with that of streaming, we developed an analytical model. We made the following simplifying assumptions to develop our model (these assumptions are relaxed in the simulation study):

1. All objects stored in the system have identical consumption rate R_c.
2. The delivery ratio

$$r = \frac{R_l}{R_c} \tag{2}$$

   is an integer.
3. Client side buffer size is greater than or equal to the object size and its transfer rate is greater than or equal to R_l .
4. Poisson inter-arrival and display duration of requests are assumed.

The 2-*Level* architecture shown in figure 1 can be modeled after the M/M/m queuing system shown in figure 4. The multimedia server is represented by the single-queue multiserver system with m = *lr* server each of which is capable of supporting R_c. With Streaming, the data is delivered at the consumption rate. Therefore, each accepted request is assigned to one and only one of the m servers in the M/M/m system. This is reflected in the state diagram shown in figure 5(a). The system has maximum queue length = 0 and thus only *lr*+1 states (requests are either accepted or rejected but never queued). The two main performance criteria we are going to investigate in this section are the probability of rejecting a request

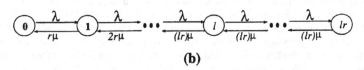

Figure 4. M/M/m queue.

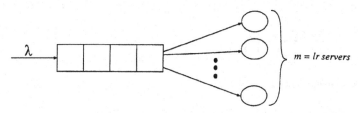

(a)

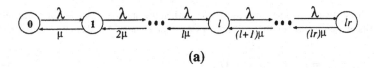

(b)

Figure 5. M/M/m queue.

P_{rej} and the server utilization. Using the state diagram in figure 5(a), both performance measures can be calculated as follows:

$$p_1 = \left(\frac{\lambda}{\mu}\right) \times p_0$$

$$p_2 = \left(\frac{\lambda}{\mu}\right)^2 \times \frac{1}{2!} p_0$$

$$p_k = \left(\frac{\lambda}{\mu}\right)^k \times \frac{1}{k!} p_0 \quad (0 < k \leq lr)$$

since,

$$\sum_{k=0}^{lr} p_k = 1$$

$$\Rightarrow$$

$$\sum_{k=0}^{lr} \left(\frac{\lambda}{\mu}\right)^k \times \frac{1}{k!} p_0 = 1$$

$$\Rightarrow$$

$$p_0 = \left[\sum_{k=0}^{lr} \left(\frac{\lambda}{\mu}\right)^k \times \frac{1}{k!}\right]^{-1}$$

So the system utilization is:

$$\rho = \sum_{k=0}^{lr} p_k \times \frac{k}{lr} = \left(\frac{\lambda}{\mu}\right)\left(\frac{1}{lr}\right) \sum_{k=0}^{lr-1} \left(\frac{\lambda}{\mu}\right)^k \times \frac{1}{k!} p_0 \tag{3}$$

Since the system starts rejecting requests only when the maximum number of concurrent requests $m = lr$ is reached, the probability of rejection equals the probability of state lr:

$$P_{rej} = P_{lr} = \left(\frac{\lambda}{\mu}\right)^{lr} \times \left(\frac{1}{(lr)!}\right) P_0 \tag{4}$$

However, with A&RA (Section 3.2), requests are assigned the maximum amount of resources possible. Since the client side buffer is assumed to be greater or equal to the object size, the first l request will be assigned the lr servers in the M/M/m system. When the $l + 1$ request arrives, the *preemptive* admission control policy will downgrade one of the active requests and reassign some of its resources to the new request. This will continue until the maximum number of concurrent requests, m, is reached (state lr in figure 5(b)). The behavior of A&RA is demonstrated by the state diagram in figure 5(b). Note that A&RA

reassigns resources of departing requests. Therefore, the server will continue to operate at its maximum capacity as long as there are l or more requests in the system. The probability of rejection and the utilization of super-streaming can be calculated as follows:

$$p_k = \left(\frac{\lambda}{r\mu}\right)^k \times \frac{1}{k!}p_0 \quad (0 < k \le l)$$

$$p_k = \left(\frac{\lambda}{lr\mu}\right)^{k-l} p_l \quad (l < k \le lr)$$

$$\sum_{k=0}^{lr} p_k = 1$$

$\Rightarrow$

$$\sum_{k=0}^{l} \left(\frac{\lambda}{r\mu}\right)^k \times \frac{1}{k!}P_0 + \sum_{k=1}^{lr-l} \left(\frac{\lambda}{lr\mu}\right)^k \times \frac{1}{l!}\left(\frac{\lambda}{r\mu}\right)^l P_0 = 1$$

$\Rightarrow$

$$P_0 = \left[\sum_{k=0}^{l} \left(\frac{\lambda}{r\mu}\right)^k \times \frac{1}{k!} + \sum_{k=1}^{lr-l} \left(\frac{\lambda}{lr\mu}\right)^k \times \frac{1}{l!}\left(\frac{\lambda}{r\mu}\right)^l\right]^{-1}$$

$\Rightarrow$ So the system utilization is:

$$\rho = \sum_{k=0}^{l} p_k \times \frac{k}{l} + \sum_{k=l+1}^{lr} p_k \tag{5}$$

and the probability of rejection is:

$$P_{rej} = P_{lr} = \left(\frac{\lambda}{lr\mu}\right)^{lr-l} \times \left(\frac{\lambda}{r\mu}\right)^l \times \frac{1}{l!}p_0 \tag{6}$$

With this analytical model, streaming can be considered as a special case of super-streaming when $r = 1$.

Trivially, the performance of the system depends on the value of r. The higher the value of r the faster it is for the multimedia server to reach its maximum delivery rate and the higher the probability that it stays at this rate. This is depicted in Tables 1 and 2. As the value of r increases, the improvement in both server utilization and probability of rejection is evidence. For example, at $Load = 85\%$ as r increases from 1 to 5 the rejection % decreases from 8.59% to 0.82%, more than a 90% improvement.

Table 1. The effect of the delivery ratio r on the server utilization.

Load (%)	$r = 1$	$r = 2$	$r = 5$	$r = 10$
55	0.5475	0.5500	0.5500	0.5500
60	0.5941	0.5999	0.6000	0.6000
65	0.6382	0.6495	0.6499	0.6500
70	0.6790	0.6988	0.6997	0.6998
75	0.7158	0.7467	0.7490	0.7493
80	0.7485	0.7927	0.7973	0.7979
85	0.7770	0.8354	0.8432	0.8445
90	0.8017	0.8734	0.8849	0.8870
95	0.8229	0.9057	0.9203	0.9232
100	0.8411	0.9318	0.9480	0.9512

Table 2. The effect of the delivery ratio r on rejection%.

Load (%)	$r = 1$	$r = 2$	$r = 5$	$r = 10$
55	0.46	0.01	0.00	0.00
60	0.98	0.02	0.00	0.00
65	1.81	0.07	0.01	0.01
70	3.00	0.19	0.04	0.03
75	4.56	0.44	0.13	0.09
80	6.44	0.91	0.34	0.26
85	8.59	1.71	0.82	0.65
90	10.92	2.95	1.68	1.45
95	13.38	4.66	3.13	2.83
100	15.89	6.82	5.20	4.88

3.5. Performance evaluation

We conducted a simulation study in order to: 1) verify our analytical mode, 2) study the impact of buffer size on the performance of the system, and 3) compare the performance of our alternative resource management policies. First, we describe our simulation setup and then report the results for each case in turn.

3.5.1. Simulation setup. Poisson distribution was used to simulate the requests' inter-arrival period. Each experiment was repeated multiple times with different seeds for the random number generators. The following system parameters were used: $R_c = 1.5$Mb/s, $R_l = 3.0$Mb/s and thus $r = 2$, average object length $= 100$ minutes, and server bandwidth $= 30$Mb/s.

To create a more realistic environment, we relaxed some of the assumptions listed in Section 3.4 as follows:

1. Object size varies from 80 to 120 minutes (with a uniform distribution).
2. Client buffer size from 0% to 100% of the average object size.

3.5.2. Simulation results. The analytical model we presented is valid only under the assumptions listed in Section 3.4. However, to compare the performance of the two delivery approaches in a more realistic environment, we built a simulation model that enabled us to relax some of these assumptions. To examine the stability of our simulation model we a number of experiments with the same assumptions we used in our analytical model and compared the two results.

Tables 3 and 4 show the comparison between our analytical and simulation results. Our analytical model can be verified by the very low value of Diff (%) (the percentage difference between the two sets of results).

Table 3. Simulation vs. analytical (streaming).

Load (%)	Server utilization			Rejection (%)		
	Analytical	Simulation	Diff (%)	Analytical	Simulation	Diff (%)
55	0.5475	0.5467	0.15	0.46	0.44	4.35
60	0.5941	0.5934	0.12	0.98	0.93	5.10
65	0.6382	0.6378	0.09	1.81	1.76	2.76
70	0.6790	0.6780	0.15	3.00	2.97	1.00
75	0.7158	0.7150	0.11	4.56	4.48	1.75
80	0.7485	0.7482	0.04	6.44	6.38	0.93
85	0.7770	0.7767	0.04	8.59	8.51	0.93
90	0.8017	0.8013	0.05	10.92	10.78	1.28
95	0.8229	0.8224	0.06	13.38	13.26	0.90
100	0.8411	0.8406	0.06	15.89	15.77	0.76

Table 4. Simulation vs. analytical (super-streaming).

Load (%)	Server utilization			Rejection (%)		
	Analytical	Simulation	Diff (%)	Analytical	Simulation	Diff (%)
55	0.5500	0.5491	0.16	0.01	0.01	0.00
60	0.5999	0.5989	0.17	0.02	0.02	0.00
65	0.6495	0.6486	0.14	0.07	0.07	0.00
70	0.6988	0.6978	0.14	0.19	0.18	5.28
75	0.7467	0.7458	0.12	0.44	0.42	4.55
80	0.7927	0.7918	0.11	0.91	0.88	3.30
85	0.8354	0.8344	0.12	1.71	1.68	1.75
90	0.8734	0.8722	0.14	2.95	2.93	0.68
95	0.9057	0.9047	0.11	4.66	4.63	0.64
100	0.9318	0.9306	0.13	6.82	6.82	0.00

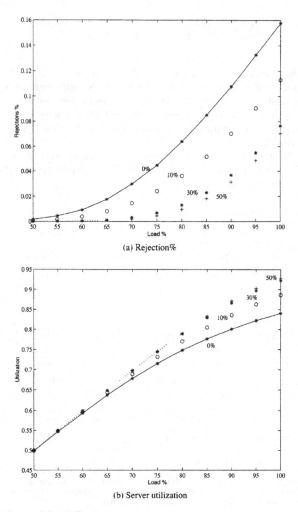

(a) Rejection%

(b) Server utilization

Figure 6. The impact of client buffer size.

Assuming a client side buffer with a size greater or equal to the object size had a major impact on the performance results obtained in Section 3.4. To understand the effect of the client buffer size on the performance of the system, we ran a number of experiments varying the buffer size from 0% to 100% of the average object size. In figure 6, the x-axis represents the system load (100% indicates that the system is operating at maximum capability). The y-axis represents the percentage of requests rejected (figure 6(a)) or server utilization (figure 6(b)) for the system employing streaming (with buffer size equaling 0% of object size) and super-streaming (with buffer size equaling 10%, 30% or 50% of object size). As expected, figure 6(a) shows that the number of rejections is inversely proportional to the client buffer size. For example, at *Load* = 85%, as the buffer size increases from 0% (streaming) to 10% and 30%, the rejection % improves by 40% and 62% respectively. The client buffer size determines the amount of data that super-stream can buffer (i.e., delivered ahead of its display). Therefore, as the client buffer size increases, the probability that idle resources are utilized by super-stream increases and thus the better performance. The corresponding increase in utilization is shown in figure 6(b).

We performed a number of experiments to evaluate the performance of our resource management policies. Figure 7 demonstrates the superiority of *A&RA* over *A&R*. Utilizing the resource of departing request maximizes server utilization thus reducing the rejection %. For example, at *Load* = 85%, A&RA rejected 35% less requests than A&R. The effect of delivery ratio r was demonstrated by the analytical model. Therefore, we elected not to investigate it further in this section. We, however, will revisit admission control policies in the performance evaluation of our *m-Level* architecture (Section 4.4).

4. *m-Level* architecture

In this section, we will generalize our *2-Level* to a multi-level architecture. With the m-level architecture, requests are submitted to a distributed server (DS) consisting of a number of centralized CM servers connected to each other via dedicated communication links [8, 33, 42]. Upon the arrival of a new request, the system has to locate a node (server) that has the requested object and the required resources to deliver the object. To deliver the CM object, with a consumption rate R_c, from the source N_s to the user N_0, the system needs to establish a *path* (figure 8).

Definition 1. A *Path* is a sequence of nodes $\langle N_s, N_{s-1}, \ldots, N_0 \rangle$. Where N_s is the source node (i.e., the node delivering the object O_k) and N_0 is the user node (i.e., the node displaying O_k).

The streaming policy will reserve R_c on all the links (and possibly the nodes) participating in a path. In this section, however, we describe an *m-Level* super-streaming policy that utilizes a higher bandwidth on the links in order to expedite the object delivery. Since the display is restricted by R_c, the policy once again needs some buffer space (disk and/or memory) at the user side and/or other intermediate nodes to store the portion which is delivered but not yet displayed.

4.1. *Resource management*

With the *2-Level* architecture, assigning resources to streams is not a very complex task. With the *m-Level* architecture, however, investigating the amount of resource that a delivery can utilize is not trivial. Therefore, we propose a more sophisticated resource management policy. The policy is designed with the following rules of thumb in mind:

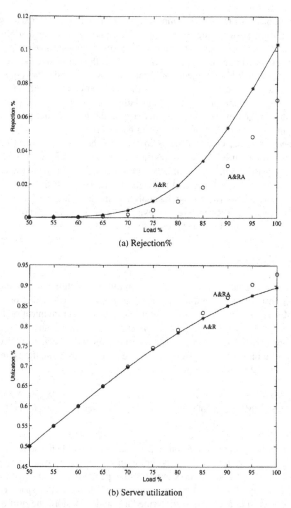

Figure 7.   Resource management policies (50% buffer size).

a. Over-committing resources can have a negative impact on the system performance and thus should be avoided.
b. Upward renegotiation of resources (i.e., a request demanding more resources after initiating the delivery) might fail and thus should be avoided. The request, however, can release some of the committed resources during the delivery.
c. The policy should strive to buffer as much data as possible as close as possible to the user. By buffering data at nodes close to the user, the policy can reduce the number of links

140

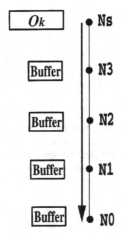

Figure 8. Delivery path.

1: Determine if the policy is applicable.

2: Identify all the bottleneck nodes (i.e., nodes along the path, including N_0, that can be utilized to buffer data for later display).

3: Compute the size of the buffer required at each bottleneck node.

4: Compute the utilized bandwidth at each link and each bottleneck node. As a result, a subset of the bottleneck nodes will be selected as buffering nodes.

5: Generate a retrieval plan that specifies which portion of the object should be buffered at which buffering node.

6: Commit the required resources and initiate the delivery.

Figure 9. The resource management policy.

needed to deliver the buffered data to the user hence reducing the overall communication cost of the delivery.

Given a path, the resource management policy goes through 6 steps (see figure 9) before starting the delivery.

4.1.1. Identifying bottleneck nodes. Given a delivery path $\langle N_s, N_{s-1}, \ldots, N_0 \rangle$, each node N_i functions both as a receiver and transmitter of a continuous media stream (except N_s and N_0). If the receiving rate of a node is higher than its transmitting rate, the node is identified

```
1.   current_flow = f_out(N_s)
2.   for i = s to 0 do
3.       f_usable(N_i) = current_flow
4.       BN(N_i) = false
5.       if current_flow > f_out(N_i)          /* flow-in exceeds flow-out */
6.           BN(N_i) = true                     /* node is flagged as a bottleneck */
7.           current_flow = f_out(N_i)          /* flow-in for the next bottleneck */
```

Figure 10.   Identifying bottleneck nodes.

as a *bottleneck* node. To match the receiving rate with the transmitting rate, the bottleneck node must store the portion of the object that is received but not yet transmitted. In this section, we describe an algorithm that identifies the bottleneck nodes (step 2 of figure 9). A by-product of this algorithm is to examine the applicability of the policy (step 1 of figure 9). We start by defining some terms.

Definition 2.   *Flow-out* of node N_i, $f_{out}(N_i)$, is the amount of available bandwidth on the link connecting N_i to its child (N_{i-1}) in a selected path.

Definition 3.   *Usable flow* of node N_i is the maximum available bandwidth from N_s to N_i or,

$$f_{usable}(N_i) = Min_{j=i+1}^{s} f_{out}(N_j) \qquad (7)$$

Definition 4. N_i is a *bottleneck* node if $f_{usable}(N_i) > f_{out}(N_i)$.

The policy needs to identify all the nodes N_i with $f_{usable}(N_i)$ exceeding $f_{out}(N_i)$. N_s can transfer to N_i more data than what N_i can send out to nodes below it in the path (N_j where $j < i$). These nodes are identified as bottleneck nodes that can be utilized by the policy to buffer part of the object.

A naive algorithm may traverse the path investigating whether each node is a bottleneck node using Eq. (7). The complexity of this approach is $O(s^2)$. Figure 10, however, shows a top-down algorithm that performs this task in $O(s)$. If f_{usable} of the first bottleneck node in the path (i.e., the closest bottleneck node to N_s) equals the display rate of the object, the path does not have any extra bandwidth hence making super-streaming inapplicable.

4.1.2. Buffer size computation.   In this section, we present two data flow paradigms for super-streams: *Sequential Data Flow* (SDF) and *Parallel Data Flow* (PDF). The computation of steps 3 and 4 of figure 9 varies depending on the employed paradigm. We only describe the computation for PDF.

The *SDF* paradigm is the intuitive way of supporting super-streams (see figure 11(a)). The buffer is concurrently being read and written by transmitting and receiving streams, respectively. Since N_i is a bottleneck node, the transmitting rate is less than the receiving rate. The buffer size is hence a function of the difference between the two rates. The disadvantage of SDF is that N_i (the server) needs to support an aggregation of transmitting and receiving rates.

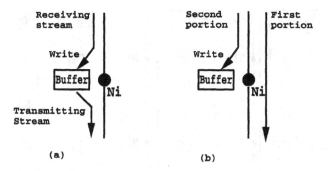

Figure 11.   SDF vs. PDF.

An alternative approach is to employ the PDF paradigm. To illustrate, let us first assume that there is only a single bottleneck node N_i in the path (see figure 11(b)). In this case, PDF conceptually breaks the object into two portions. The first portion is delivered to the user directly, bypassing the bottleneck node. The second portion of the object is written to the buffer simultaneously with the delivery of the first portion. By careful computation of the size of each portion of the object, PDF can guarantee that the second portion becomes entirely resident in the buffer prior to the completion of the delivery of the first portion. Consequently, the flow can continue with no interruptions by delivering the second portion of the object to the user from the buffer. Trivially, the buffer size is equal to the size of the second portion and is computed by modifying Eq. (1) as:

$$buffer\_size = \frac{(f_{achievable}(N_i) - f_{out}(N_i)) * O_k.size}{f_{achievable}(N_i)} \qquad (8)$$

where $f_{achievable}$ is the maximum rate that N_i can handle and is dominated by either the rate of the incoming link or the server bandwidth ($SR_{bw}(N_i)$). That is,

Definition 5.   Achievable flow of a bottleneck node N_i is the maximum amount of bandwidth that N_i can receive without data loss or,

$$f_{achievable}(N_i) = Min(f_{usable}(N_i), SR_{bw}(N_i) + f_{out}(N_i)) \qquad (9)$$

The buffer size computed by Eq. (8) is the optimal buffer size. However, this optimal buffer size might exceed the server available storage capacity ($SR_{cap}(N_i)$). In this case, PDF fixes the size of the second portion as $SR_{cap}(N_i)$ and computes the size of the first portion accordingly. Since $SR_{cap}(N_i)$ is less than the buffer size computed by Eq. (8), the delivery of first portion completes only after the buffer is filled with the second portion. The only problem is that the second portion will now reside in the buffer for a longer duration of time. This is because the size of the first portion is now larger and hence it requires a longer time

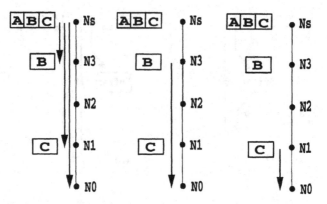

Figure 12. Recursive object partitioning.

to deliver. We can remedy this situation by reducing the transmission rate of the second portion correspondingly. Due to lack of space, we will not investigate this optimization any further.

If there are more than one bottleneck node in a path, then the above procedure will be applied recursively to the first portion of the object. To illustrate, consider figure 12 with path $\langle N_s, N_3, N_2, N_1, N_0 \rangle$ where N_3 and N_1 are bottleneck nodes. Assume the three consecutive portions of the object are A, B and C. PDF is a bottom-up algorithm. Therefore, it starts with bottleneck N_1 and breaks the object into two portions: AB and C. AB will be scheduled to be delivered directly to the user while C will be delivered to the buffer at N_1. Subsequently, the recursion applies to AB and bottleneck N_3. That is, A is delivered directly to the user and B becomes a resident of N_3's buffer. This recursive partitioning of the object (figure 12) will result in early releasing of the resources as opposed to any alternative partitioning method.

Figure 13 depicts a complete algorithm to compute both the required buffer size and $f_{achievable}$ per each bottleneck node in the path (step 3 and 4 in figure 9) in $O(s)$. This algorithm will also generate a delivery plan (step 5 in figure 9) consistent with the above mentioned recursive partitioning. After deciding on the subobjects assignment, the resources are committed and the super-stream is initiated (step 6 in figure 9).

4.2. Admission control

Unlike our 2-level architecture, clients in the m-level architecture compete for a number of resources making admission control more challenging. Once again a newly arriving request may need resources that are utilized by super-streams to buffer part(s) of objects. The system may employ a *non-preemptive* policy and reject the request or *preemptive*

```
1.    Subobject_size = $O_k.size$
2.    current_achievable_flow = $f_{usable}(N_0)$
3.    for node = $N_0$ to $N_s$ do
4.        $f_{achievable}(N_i)$ = current_achievable_flow
5.        if $BN(N_i)$ == true                                    /* if a bottleneck node */
6.            if $(f_{achievable}(N_i) - f_{out}(N_i)) > SR_{bw}(N_i)$
7.                $f_{achievable}(N_i) = SR_{bw}(N_i) + f_{out}(N_i)$          /* Eq.  9 */
8.            buffer_size = $[(f_{achievable}(N_i) - f_{out}(N_i))$ * Suboject_size]
9.                / $f_{achievable}(N_i)$                          /* Eq.  1 */
10.           current_achievable_flow = $f_{achievable}(N_i)$
11.           if buffer_size > $SR_{cap}(N_i)$
12.               $SR_{achievable}N_i = SR_{cap}(N_i)$             /*buffer size to be utilized */
13.           else $SR_{achievable}N_i$ = buffer_size
14.           Subobject_size = Subobject_size - $SR_{achievable}N_i$
```

Figure 13. Buffer size calculation with PDF.

policy and attempt to accept the request by downgrading other super-streams. However, investigating if downgrading one or more super-streams will free enough resources to admit the new request and deciding which super-stream to downgrade if more than on exist is not trivial.

In our performance evaluation, we have measured the performance of the system with both the *preemptive* and *non-preemptive* policies. In our implementation, when a new request arrives and the system does not have enough resources to accept it, the *preemptive* admission control policy, attempts to allocate resources by downgrading the most recently admitted super-streaming delivery. Currently, we are implementing the *preemptive* admission control policy with different heuristics to select which super-stream to downgrade if more than one exists.

4.3. Multiple delivery rates

Applying our multiple delivery rates in the m-level architecture is slightly different. With the m-level architecture, the buffer size calculation algorithm (Section 4.1.2) partitions the object into n portions (not necessarily equal). When the start of portion q falls into an occupied slot, the system compensates by shifting the start of the this portion to the first available slot. However, to avoid overflowing the buffer at any of the bottleneck nodes, this shift must be propagated to all the portions $q - i > 1$. Hence, increasing the size of only the first portion.

4.4. Performance evaluation

We conducted a number of simulation experiments to obtain some insights about the performance of DS with both super-streaming and streaming. We elected to build a simple model that consist of 4 nodes simulating a path in DS (similar to figure 8). By doing so, we were able to neutralize other issues related to DS (for more on these issues see [42]) and focus on

Table 5. System parameters.

Node	Server capacity (GB)	Server bandwidth (Mb/s)	Link bandwidth (Mb/s)
1	8	100	50
2	12	200	100
3	20	200	100
4	50	200	Ø

the object delivery problem. To better evaluate super-streaming in the m-level architecture, we forced the system to deliver the object to the user at the consumption rate R_c. By doing so, we can ensure that any improvement in performance is not due to client side buffering but rather due to applying super-streaming at intermediate nodes. The parameters of the model are detailed in Table 5.

A static object population was assumed: all objects were stored at the highest node in the path, and no new objects are inserted during the execution of the simulation. Popular objects are replicated at other nodes according to the LFU replacement policy presented in [42]. In addition, objects had random size and bandwidth requirement. A request only arrives at the head-end node (N_1 in figure 8), and subsequently, it is either served immediately, or rejected if its required resources are not available.

Poisson distribution was used to simulate the requests' inter-arrival period. To simulate object selections, Zipf's law [33] was employed. Each experiment was repeated multiple times with different seeds for the random number generators. To simulate multiple requests sharing intermediate nodes and links, we devised an artificial load generator.

We will present two performance comparisons to give a flavor of the improvement achieved by applying our super-streaming paradigm. In figure 14, the x-axis represents the system load (100% indicates that the system is operating at maximum capability). The y-axis represents the number of requests rejected by the system employing streaming and super-streaming (with 20% of the servers capacity used for buffering and the rest for storing regular objects). As expected, super-streaming employing a non-preemptive admission control policy rejected more requests than streaming. On the other hand, super-streaming employing a preemptive admission control policy observed approximately 30% to 10% less rejections than streaming under medium system load ($30\% \leq load \leq 70\%$).

At higher system load ($85\% \leq load$), however, super-streaming starts to reject more requests. By designating some of the head-end server capacity as a buffer space, the system reduces the number of objects stored in this head-end. As a result, more requests are forced to retrieve objects from higher nodes in the path thus increasing the overall network requirement of the system. At medium load, the improvement in performance gained by applying super-streaming compensates for this increase. At higher load, however, the system resources are approaching saturation which leaves no extra resources for super-streaming to utilize. Therefore, the number of requests rejected by super-streaming becomes higher than that of streaming.

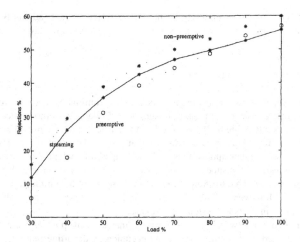

Figure 14. Throughput (super-streaming vs. streaming).

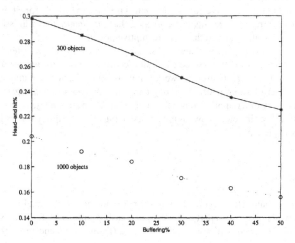

Figure 15. Head-end hits.

The effect of buffer size on the number of requests served by the head-end is demonstrated in figure 15. The figure shows the head-end hit percentage (the percentage of requests served by the head-end) as a function of buffering percentage (the percentage of server capacity designated for buffering) for our system storing 300 and 1000 objects. As the buffering percentage increases, the number of objects stored in the head-end decreases, thus reducing the number of requests served by it. However, the rate of reduction is lower for the system

147

with 1000 objects, since the popularity of the objects stored in the head-end is inversely proportional to the total number of objects stored in the system (Zipf's law).

5. Conclusions and future research

We proposed a super-streaming paradigm which allows continuous media servers to utilize resources, that are otherwise unused, to support a display. We demonstrated how this paradigm can be employed in both the 2-level and the m-level architectures. Furthermore, we presented a multiple delivery rate technique that is not only essential for our paradigm but can be utilized by other applications. We developed an analytical and a simulation model that demonstrated the superiority of super-streaming over streaming. With the analytical model, we were able to show the effect of delivery ratio r on the performance of super-streaming. Moreover, with the simulation study, we demonstrated how the increase in client buffer size impacts the system performance.

With super-streaming, two alternative resource management policies were proposed. Since $A\&RA$ utilized the resources previously occupied by departing requests, it outperformed $A\&R$ (rejected 35% less request at $Load = 85\%$). In addition, we presented a preemptive and a non-preemptive admission control policies to provide for a fair treatment of requests. Our simulation results demonstrated that the preemptive admission control policy significantly outperformed the non-preemptive policy.

This study can be extended in many ways. As short term plans, we intend to design heuristics that can be employed by the admission control policies to improve the performance of super-streaming. Currently, we are investigating delivery techniques that can support non-integer multiple rates. As a long term plan, we want to investigate new challenges introduced by other applications when assuming super-streaming. For example, the temporal relationships introduced by digital editing applications or query scripts introduced by MM-DBMS applications.

Acknowledgment

We would like to thank Hezhi Ai for helping us with the analytical model of Section 3.4. This research was supported in part by unrestricted cash/equipment gifts from NCR, Intel, JPL contract 9529152 and NSF grants EEC-9529152 (IMSC ERC) and MRI-9724567.

Notes

1. In this paper, we assume constant bit-rate (CBR) (i.e., the display bandwidth R_c of a single object is fixed for the entire display duration). To support variable bit-rate objects, a CBR system can employ one of the techniques described in [1].
2. Although other types of connections are possibles, ADSL appears to be the strongest candidate [8].
3. We discuss the act of getting back resources from an active request (i.e., downgrading) as part of our admission control policy in Section 3.3.

References

1. J. Al-Marri and S. Ghandeharizadeh, "An evaluation of alternative disk scheduling techniques in support of variable bit rate continuous media," in EDBT98,Valencia, Spain, March 1998.
2. D. Anderson and G. Homsy, "A cotinuous media I/O server and its synchronization," IEEE Computer, October 1991.
3. P.B. Berra, F. Golshani, R. Mehrotra, and O.R.L. Sheng, "Multimedia information systems," IEEE Transactions on Knowledge and Data Engineering, Vol. 5, No. 4, 1993.
4. S. Berson, S. Ghandeharizadeh, R. Muntz, and X. Ju, "Staggered striping in multimedia information systems," in Proceedings of the ACM SIGMOD International Conference on Management of Data, 1994, pp. 79–89.
5. S. Berson, L. Golubchik, and R.R. Muntz, "A fault tolerant design of a multimedia server," in Proceedings of the ACM SIGMOD International Conference on Management of Data, 1995, pp. 364–375.
6. E. Biersack and F. Thiesse, "Statistical admission control in video servers with constant data length retrieval of vbr streams," in Third International Conference on Multimedia Modeling, Toulouse, France, November 1996.
7. C. Bisdikian and B. Patel, "Issues on movie allocation in distributed video-on-demand systems," in IEEE International Conference on Communications, June 1995.
8. C. Bisdikian and B. Patel, "Cost-based program allocation for distributed multimedia-on-demand systems," IEEE MultiMedia, pp. 62–72, Fall 1996.
9. J.F. Buford (Ed.), Multimedia Systems, Addison-Wesley, 1994.
10. E. Chang and H. Carcia-Molina, "Efficient memory use in a media server," in Proceedings of the International Conference on Very Large Databases, 1997.
11. E. Chang and H. Garcia-Molina, "Medic: A memory and disk cache for multimedia clients," Technical Report SIDL-WP-1997-0076, Stanford University, 1997.
12. H.J. Chen and T. Little, "Physical storage organizations for time-dependent multimedia data," in Proceedings of the Foundations of Data Organization and Algorithms (FODO) Conference, October 1993.
13. M. Chen and D.D. Kandlur, "Stream conversion to support interactive video playout," IEEE Multimedia, Summer 1996.
14. W. Chen and D. Waring, "Applicability of ADSL to support video dial tone in copper loopi," IEEE Communication Magazine, pp. 102–109, May 1994.
15. S.M. Chung (Ed.), Multimedia Information Storage and Management, Kluwer Academic Publishers, 1996.
16. J. Dengler, S. Stavros, and E. Biersack, "Deterministic admission control strategies on video servers with variable bit rate streams," in European Workshop on Interactive Distributed Multimedia Systems and Telecommunication Services IDMS97, Heidelberg, Germany, March 1996.
17. M. Franklin, M. Carey, and M. Livny, "Local disk caching for client-server database systems," VLDB, August 1993.
18. B. Furht, D. Kalra, F. Kitson, A. Rodriguez, and W. Wall, "Design issues for interactive television systems," Computer, pp. 25–39, May 1995.
19. J. Gecsei, "Adaptation in distributed multimedia systems," IEEE MultiMedia, pp. 58–66, April–June 1997.
20. D.J. Gemmell and S. Christodoulakis, "Principles of delay sensitive multimedia data storage and rtrieval," ACM Trans. Information Systems, Vol. 10, No. 1, pp. 51–90, 1992.
21. D.J. Gemmell, H.M. Vin, D.D. Kandlur, P.V. Rangan, and L.A. Rowe, "Multimedia storage servers: A tutorial," IEEE Computer, May 1995.
22. A. Ghafoor, "Special issue on multimedia database systems," ACM Multimedia Systems, Vol. 3, Nos. 5/6, 1995.
23. S. Ghandeharizadeh, S.H. Kim, and C. Shahabi, "On disk scheduling and data placement for video serers," USC Technical Report, University of Southern California, 1996.
24. S. Ghandeharizadeh, R. Zimmermann, W. Shi, R. Rejaie, D. Ierardi, and T.W. Li, "Mitra: A scalable continuous media server," Kluwer Multimedia Tools and Applications, January 1997.
25. W. Grosky, R. Jain, and R. Mehrotra (Ed.), The Handbook of Multimedia Information Management, Prentice-Hall, 1997.
26. D. Harman, G. Huang, G. Im, M. Nguyen, J. Werner, and M. Wong, "Local distribution for imtv," IEEE MultiMedia, pp. 14–23, Fall 1995.

27. J. Hsieh, M. Lin, J.C.L. Liu, and D.H.C. Du, "Performance of a mass storage system for video-on-demand," Journal of Parallel and Distributed Computing on Multimedia Processing and Technology, to appear.
28. J. Huang, Y. Wang, N. Vaidyanathan, and F. Cao, "Grms: A global resource management systems for distributed QoS and criticality support," in IEEE Int'l Conf. on Multimedia Computing and Systems (ICMCS'97), June 1997.
29. T. Little and D. Venkatesh, "Prospects for interactive video-on-demand," IEEE MultiMedia, pp. 14–24, Fall 1994.
30. D. Makaroff, G. Neufeld, and N. Hutchinson, "An evaluation of VBR disk admission algorithms for continuous media file servers" in Fifth ACM Conference on Multimedia, November 1997.
31. C. Martin, P.S. Narayan, B. Özden, R. Rastogi, and A. Silberschatz, "The fellini multimedia storage server," in Multimedia Information Storage and Management, ch. 5. Kluwer Academic Publishers, Boston, August 1996, ISBN: 0-7923-9764-9.
32. K. Nahrstedt, "Resource management in networked multimedia systems," Computer, pp. 52–63, May 1995.
33. J. Nussbaumer, B. Patel, F. Schaffa, and J. Sterbenz, "Network requirements for interactive video on demand," IEEE Journal on Selected Areas in Communications, Vol. 13, No. 5, pp. 779–787, 1995.
34. K. Nwosu, B. Thuraisingham, and P.B. Berra, "Multimedia database systems—A new frontier," IEEE MultiMedia, Vol. 4, No. 3, pp. 21–23, 1997.
35. K. Patel, D. Simpson, D. Wu, and L. Rowe, "Synchornized continuous media playback through the world wide web," ACM Multimedia, November 1996.
36. M. Prycker, Asynchronous Transfer Mode: Solution for Broadband ISDN, Prentice Hall International: UK, 1995.
37. S. Ramanathan and P. Rangan, "Architectures for personalized multimedia," IEEE MultiMedia, pp. 37–46, Spring 1994.
38. P. Rangan and H. Vin, "Efficient storage techniques for digital continuous media," IEEE Transactions on Knowledge and Data Engineering, Vol. 5, No. 4, 1993.
39. P. Rangan, H. Vin, and S. Ramanathan, "Designing an on-demand multimeida service," IEEE Communications Magazine, Vol. 30, No. 7, 1992.
40. A.L.N. Reddy and J.C. Wyllie, "I/O issues in a multimedia system," IEEE Computer Magazine, Vol. 27, No. 3, pp. 69–74, 1994.
41. D. Reiniger, D. Raychaudhuri, B. Melamed, B. Sengupta, and J. Hill, "Statical multiplexing of VBR MPEG compressed video on ATM network," IEEE INFOCOM, March 1993.
42. C. Shahabi, M. Alshayeji, and S. Wang, "A redundant hierarchical structure for a distributed continuous media server," in Fourth European Workshop on Interactive Distributed Multimedia Systems and Telecommunication Services IDMS97, Darmstadt, Germany, September 1997.
43. H. Stuttgen, "Network evolution and multimedia communication," IEEE MultiMedia, pp. 42–59, Fall 1995.
44. V.S. Subrahmanian and S. Jajodia (Eds.), Multimedia Database Systems, Springer, 1996.
45. W. Tavanapong, K.A. Hua, and J.Z. Wang, "A framework for supporting previewing and vcr operations in a low bandwidth environment," in ACM Multimedia, November 1997.
46. F.A. Tobagi, J. Pang, R. Baird, and M. Gang, "Streaming RAID—A disk array management system for video files," in First ACM Conference on Multimedia, August 1993.
47. H. Vin and P. Rangan, "Designing a multiuser HDTV storage server," IEEE Journal on Selected Areas in Communications, Vol. 11, No. 1, pp. 153–164, 1993.
48. W. Wolf, Y. Liang, M. Kozuch, H. Yu, M. Phillips, M. Weekes, and A. Debruyne, "A digital video library of the world wide web," ACM Multimedia, November 1996.
49. D. Worsley, "Isochronous etherner—An ATM bridge for multimedia networking," IEEE MultiMedia, pp. 58–67, January–March 1997.
50. C. Wu, G. Ma, and B. Lin, "Optimization of downstream delivery on catv network," in IEEE Int'l Conf. on Communications, 1996.
51. P.S. Yu, M.-S. Chen, and D.D. Kandlur, "Grouped sweeping scheduling for DASD-based multimedia storage management," Multimedia Systems, Vol. 1, No. 1, pp. 99–109, 1993.

Cyrus Shahabi is currently a Research Assistant Professor and the Director of the Distributed Information Management Laboratory at the Computer Science Department and the Integrated Media Systems Center (IMSC) at the University of Southern California. He received his Ph.D. degree in Computer Science at the University of Southern California in August 1996. He participated in the design and the implementation of the Omega object oriented parallel database machine. Dr. Shahabi's current research interests include Multimedia Databases and Storage Servers, Internet and Distributed Databases, Data Mining, and Query Optimization. He has served as a referee for prestigious database conferences (e.g., SIGMOD, VLDB) and journals (e.g., IEEE TKDE). He is serving as a program committee member for DEXA 1997–99, ACM WIDM 98, SPIE'98 and ACM CIKM'99 conferences. He is also the chair of ACM WIDM'99.

Mohammad Alshayeji is a doctoral candidate in the Department of Computer Science at the University of Southern California. He received his M.S. degree in Computer Science from the University of Central Florida in 1995. His research interest includes distributed multimedia systems, multimedia databases, and video-on-demand.